LOST CHINA

TRAVEL CLASSICS FROM THE AGES

Edited by
GRAHAM EARNSHAW

EARNSHAW
BOOKS

Lost China: Travel Classics from the Ages

Edited by Graham Earnshaw

ISBN-13: 978-988-8552-12-2

This book has been reset in 10pt Book Antiqua. Spellings and punctuations are left as in the original edition.

HISTORY / Asia / China

EB094

Published by Earnshaw Books Ltd. (Hong Kong)

CONTENTS

FOREWORD   vii

CHAPTER 1   1
Aeneas Anderson
A Narrative of the British Embassy to China
1792-1794

CHAPTER 2   22
Évariste Régis Huc
A Journey through the Chinese Empire

CHAPTER 3   57
Laurence Oliphant
Elgin's Mission to China and Japan

CHAPTER 4   75
John "China" Thomson
Illustrations of China and It's People

CHAPTER 5   100
Oscar Terry Crosby
Tibet & Turkestan

CHAPTER 6   124
Elizabeth Kendall
A Wayfarer in China: Impressions of a Trip Across West China
and Mongolia

CHAPTER 7   149
Mary Gaunt
A Broken Journey

CHAPTER 8   170
Roy Andrews
Camps and Trails in China

FOREWORD

THE INITIAL REASON for founding Earnshaw Books in 2004 was that I had found so many books written in the past by foreigners traveling or living in China that, while shining with vibrancy and fascinating detail, had been forgotten by the world. The aim was take some of these wonderful books off the dusty shelves and give them another run in the sun.

Earnshaw Books today mostly publishes new original books, mostly still about China, but we still do some reprints of the old classics, lovingly proofed and re-set. Some of these books, it is true, can be a bit turgid, a trifle difficult to get through for various reasons. So a few decades ago — somewhere around 1982. I wrote summaries of two of my favorite China travel books — one by a French missionary surnamed Huc who traversed most of China in the 1830s, and the other by Laurence Oliphant, who witnessed the entire second Opium War in the 1850s. Both books are immensely readable, full of great descriptions and writing, and having done than, I decided to expand on the idea and commissioned other writers to take the same summary approach with some other classics of China travel. The result is this book.

Graham Earnshaw
China
2018

1

AENEAS ANDERSON

A NARRATIVE OF THE BRITISH EMBASSY TO CHINA

BEFORE THE MACARTNEY EMBASSY set off for China in 1792, European trade with China was not, in the eyes of the tea-thirsty British, a happy venture. Tariffs were high, trade was heavily restricted and any expansion of operations was near impossible. Wanting to substantially improve these conditions, King George III, with the sincerest of blessings of the East India Company, sent Lord Macartney and a sprawling retinue to China for what would become the first major Sino-European diplomatic event. (A previous attempt was cut short when Lord Cathcart, the Ambassador, died en route.)

Officially, Macartney was not going to China on business; rather, he was armed with over six-hundred cases of luxurious gifts, going the distance to extend heartfelt congratulations on the eightieth birthday of Qianlong, the Manchu Emperor. Of course, both sides were aware that the British were angling for more than a slice of birthday cake and they arrived with a carefully drawn-up list of proposals, including permission to set up a permanent legation in the closed city of Peking, possession of an island near Chusan (an island off Shanghai) for storage and shipping, and fewer restrictions on trade.

On a birthday-party level, things appeared to go smoothly:

both the Emperor and the Ambassador were cordial and accommodating, offering each other with gifts and respect, and working to overcome cultural barriers that would have been insurmountable for lesser men. After delicate negotiations, an agreement was reached allowing Macartney to kneel before the Emperor (as he would for a British monarch) instead of kowtowing.

But despite the careful ballet of diplomacy, the Emperor was not remotely interested in changing Britain's trading status and not one of their demands was met. The Embassy was dismissed from Peking and returned to Britain on short notice. Business-wise, the mission had been a complete failure.

Present on the this trip was Macartney's valet, Aeneas Anderson, who published his own narrative of the trip published in 1795, soon after returning to Britain, with the ghost-writing help of a top hack writer of that era, William Coombe. Peppered with gossip, gripes about the "management" and informed speculation about the closed-door negotiations with the Manchu officials, Anderson's "below stairs" book is an engaging account of an historic event.

The Macartney Embassy to China set sail from Portsmouth amidst much fanfare on September 21, 1792. While their ships were some of the Empire's finest and more than capable of cruising along at a fair clip, their progress was frequently interrupted by diplomatic stops en route. Not three weeks after setting out, Anderson bemoaned that they had to stop off in Madeira for over a week so that Macartney could be adequately wined and dined by local leaders. With appetites and diplomatic gestures determining the schedule, it was almost six months before they reached their major refueling point, Batavia (present day Jakarta) in the Dutch East Indies.

Anderson, charged with organizing Macartney's baggage and arranging his lodgings, settled Macartney into his Batavian accommodations and then explored the city.

He found the Dutch architecture charming, but there was little else for him to praise. The tropical swamp climate and the stinking canals cruelly taxed the health of residents, and he reported that, "Not one in twenty of the military who came from Europe, ever returned there; and that even those who escape from hence and survive all the dangers and disorders of the climate, generally go back to their own country with emaciated forms and debilitated conditions."

On one morning in the city, he saw an elderly Malay staff member in the hotel nearly beaten to death for the omission of a minor duty. He brought the case to the attention of the Dutch hotel manager, who said "that the Malays were so extremely wicked, that neither the house nor anyone in it would be safe for a moment if they were not kept in a state of continual terror by the most rigid and exemplary punishment."

It was in Batavia that Anderson had his first glimpse of Chinese settlements: immigrants inhabiting the artisanal and manufacturing suburbs of the city. On the one hand, he liked their industrious nature and willingness to carry out work that "the Europeans through a foolish and unpardonable pride, consider[ed] as beneath them to perform", yet he found their settlements repulsive, "a scattered mass of deformity and confusion," which made him rather nervous about what he might find in China.

Two months later, the Embassy stopped at a small but unnamed island off the coast of Cochin China (today's Vietnam). Isolated and impoverished, the island was in no position to wine and dine their new guests in style. Unperturbed, Macartney went ashore to bargain with the local mandarin for meat and fruit for his hungry crew. The mandarin agreed to provide rations, and Anderson in return treated the "natives" to a display of musket fire, blasting away most of a coconut tree, as they watched on with "extreme amazement". But when the British returned the following day to collect the food, the village had been abandoned. A short letter from the mandarin informed them that they did not actually have any meat or fruit (he just wanted to avoid losing face) and, being afraid of being blasted with muskets themselves, the entire village had decamped. The mandarin also implored the visitors to please not burn down their huts, as they lacked the resources to rebuild. The obliging, if still ravenous, British left the village intact and headed onwards.

Their first point of arrival in China was Chusan (the Zhoushan Islands near Shanghai), where they were flattered to receive elaborately choreographed welcoming ceremonies greeting "His Excellency". This was followed by a socially awkward dinner on Macartney's ship with several mandarins, as it was discovered the Chinese officials did not know how to use knives and forks. But the embarrassment was soon forgotten when he was tasked with ensuring the successful transfer of the six-hundred cases of gifts for the Emperor into a fleet of Chinese junks bound for Peking.

At this point, the party was introduced to their official mandarin "handler", Van-Tadge-In. While other accounts of the Macartney mission have not always been kind to Van-Tadge-In, Anderson found his assistance with the domestic arrangements outstanding and took his presence as an auspicious sign for the Embassy's outcome.

"The appointment of such a man, so admirably qualified to fulfil the peculiar duties to which he was nominated, gave us a very favourable opinion of the good sense of the Chinese government, and served to encourage our hopes of success in the important objects of this distinguished embassy," he said.

With such a dependable Chinese counterpart, the transfer of gifts went smoothly and Anderson finally had time to relax and admire the scenery.

He was impressed by Chinese gardening techniques and the prosperous villas that he spied from the deck ("prospects of such peculiar novelty and beauty as would baffle any attempts of mine to describe them"); he found the sound of gongs (which "resembled in some degree the cover of a large stew pan") novel and fascinating, if not quite harmonious enough to consider "music"; and though he wasn't impressed with the savory cuisine, he consumed Chinese sweets and wine ("well understood by the Chinese") with abandon. With a valet's knowing assessment, and no doubt still feeling the sting from the incident in Cochin China, he reported with satisfaction that the rations provided by the Chinese were "infinitely beyond the possibility of being consumed by those alone for whose use it was presented." His most enthusiastic comments were on the local turnout, noting that "the crowds of people which assembled to see [our] parade [of junks] were beyond all calculation and almost beyond belief!"

As the party continued upriver, a heavy heat set in, followed quickly by choking clouds of mosquitoes. While Macartney and others retreated from to their private quarters – coming out only for receptions with local mandarins – Anderson braved the elements diligently remained on the observation deck. The locals continued to come out in droves to see the British:

"It may appear to be a continual repetition of the same subject, but the circumstances appeared to be so extraordinary, that I cannot fail to repeat it, by observing that, at this place, the people who covered the banks of the river, far exceeded in number anything that we had yet seen."

On August 16, 1793, the British Embassy's fleet of junks arrived at Tong-tchew, just a short overland hop from Peking. While the bigwigs were quickly escorted to more comfortable quarters in a local temple, Anderson was tasked with overseeing the safe transfer of the voluminous cargo. He was pleased to learn that special sheds and a tagging system had already been prepared, and Anderson's Chinese counterpart guided him through this organizational triumph, although his suspicions were slightly aroused when the Chinese explained they would be sending a full report of the documented items to the Emperor.

Anderson turned his nose up at the lodgings in Tong-tchew which, in a one-storey building, did not seem fitting for "his Lordship". All meals were served with "neither table-cloths or forks and knives, [but] small pointed lengths of wood, or ivory, in the form of pencils", and the Chinese giggled at the Embassy's clumsy use of chopsticks. In the face of such "slights", Macartney demanded that he be attended by armed guards to better display his station. He was assigned an interior courtyard where no one would be able to see him, but "these sentinels were placed at the outer gate, and the entrance of the inner court, that they might attract the notice of the Chinese, and elevate the consequence of the diplomatic mission, in the general opinion of the people of the country."

A member of the party – Mr. Harry Eades – died in Tong-tchew, and in order to give the Chinese "a favorable impression even of our funeral solemnities", Macartney announced that they would hold a lavish burial with full military honors, something Mr. Eades would probably not have received in Britain. With no cleric on hand to read the service, Anderson the valet was pressed into the role of Church of England minister. Whether their Chinese handlers were impressed by such antics is unclear.

The next day, the Embassy headed for Peking. The Chinese

were again prepared for their arrival, with 400 coolies on hand and organizational methods in force that went well beyond those Anderson's team usually employed. Anderson lavished praise on the Chinese for their assistance.

One obstacle neither side had anticipated were the enormous crowds of curious onlookers, which at times entirely blocked the road and had to be literally ploughed out of the way by Chinese soldiers. Anderson was sorely embarrassed by the laughter and stares of many of the onlookers, and he complained that the Embassy was not being presented in a dignified enough manner, thereby becoming an object of Chinese derision. In his opinion, the dress of the attendants was mismatched and tattered, and far too little care had been taken to arrange everyone neatly in the wagons. He was convinced the guffaws of the crowd became louder as they approached Peking. Thoroughly annoyed, Anderson said this of their arrival:

"At 2 o'clock we arrived at the gates of the grand imperial city of Pekin with very little semblance of diplomatic figure or importance: in short, for I cannot help repeating the sentiment, the appearance of the Ambassador's attendants, both with respect to the shabbiness of their dress and to the vehicles which conveyed them bore a greater resemblance to the removal of paupers to their parishes in England, than the expected dignity of the representative of a great and powerful monarch."

Anderson's concerns were forgotten as the reality of his entry into Peking began to soak in. The convoy passed through the center of the city as they had been assigned to accommodation at the Emperor's summer palace outside the city at Yuanmingyuan – but the route allowed them to take in Peking's scenery, something very few Western eyes had ever seen. Anderson described Peking as a city of admirable cleanliness and order, where industry not dissimilar from that in London thrived.

While the uniform grey, single-story architecture was foreign to him, he was delighted with familiar sights like auctions, street vendors, police headquarters and butcher shops. Of the latter, he wrote: "I observed a great number of butcher shops whose mode of cutting up their meat resembles our own; nor can the markets of London boast a better supply of flesh than is to be found in Pekin."

He was further distracted by the sight of the lovely Manchu women he glimpsed in the crowd. Anderson clearly fancied himself a bit of a lady's man and often commented on those he encountered along the trip. At one point during his visit to Peking, he even managed to escape from the convoy and have a hands-on encounter with several Chinese maidens.

"Perceiving a number of women in the crowd that surrounded us, I ventured to approach them; and addressing them with the Chinese word chou-au (or beautiful), they appeared to be extremely diverted, and gathering round me, but with an air of great modesty and politeness, they examined the make and form of my clothes, as well as the texture of the materials of which they were composed...I took leave of these obliging females with a gentle shake of the hand, which they tendered to me with the most graceful affability." As he was whisked away by his Chinese handlers, he was not able to ascertain whether his advances had caused trouble, but claimed: "the men who were present [did not] appear to be at all dissatisfied with my conduct."

Several hours later, Anderson and his colleagues arrived at the Yuanmingyuan, later called in English the "Old Summer Palace". This was supposed to be the most glorious of all the Emperor's palaces, and it was considered an enormous privilege for the Embassy to be allowed to glimpse it, let alone be housed there.

They were not, however, impressed, with Anderson

reporting: "The position of this palace is not only low but in a swampy hollow and between two pools of stagnant water, whose putrid exhalations cannot add to the comfort of this unwholesome situation [and it is also] unworthy the resident of the representative of a great monarch, not only destitute of elegance, but in a wretched state of repair."

Furthermore, the perimeter of the palace grounds was ringed with armed guards and none were allowed to exit. Chafing at both the containment and the ill-equipped quarters, Macartney demanded via his intermediaries that they be moved elsewhere, a decision that met with Anderson's approval. Ever-conscious of the image they projected to their hosts, Anderson also condemned the leadership of the Embassy for not better reigning in the British troops and held that they should abide by the Chinese rules, no matter how onerous, during their time at the Summer Palace. One of the heads of the expedition, Colonel Benson, had tried to lead a revolt against the guards and "escape" from the compound. Anderson advised a different course:

"It would perhaps have been more discreet to have spared those menaces which were continually expressed against persons charged with an official duty, and acting under the direction of their superiors; and to have submitted with patience to those regulations, which, however unpleasant, were such as were adopted by and might be the usage of, that government, whose partial favour and friendship it was the interest, and therefore the duty of the British embassy, by insinuating address and political manoeuvre, to obtain and establish."

Before the situation became explosive, the British Embassy were moved to more commodious quarters in the city center, in the sprawling palace of the Viceroy of Canton, known to English traders by the nickname John Tuck and now in prison on charges of embezzlement of public funds. These quarters they found to be much more agreeable. Amongst other amenities, the mansion had under-floor heating.

"Beneath the floor, in each of the principal apartments, is a stove, or furnace of brick-work, with a circular tribe that is conducted round the room where it stands, which is sufficient also to warm the apartment above it."

After they had settled in, Macartney received a number of mandarins, a group including several French Jesuit Priests, out of uniform as they were forbidden from promoting their religion by order of the Emperor. But "on account of their ;learning", they had been allowed to remain in Peking and had been elevated to the rank of mandarin, "These French gentlemen, who were, as may be very readily conceived, well acquainted with the interests of the country in which they were now naturalized, encouraged Lord Macartney to hope for the most satisfactory and beneficial issue of the embassy which he conducted."

The next day, an official arrived to inform that Macartney that the Emperor had invited hm for an audience at his estate in Jehol, northeast of Peking, where he was currently residing. The British rejoiced, convinced they were destined to succeed.

Preparations for the journey were particularly taxing for Anderson. This time Macartney and his inner circle had already made some "surprise" arrangements – and their "assistance" left Anderson fuming. Complaining that until now the party had looked bedraggled, Macartney announced that they had special "uniforms" for all those accompanying him to Jehol and proceeded to distribute a trunk full of green and yellow outfits to the serving classes. Anderson was interested in improving their image, but appalled by these particular uniforms. With scorn, he noted that these were not "real" uniforms but garish second-hand costumes from a fancy dress ball in London several years earlier (evidenced by the name tags sewn into them) and – to make matters worse – they only came in very large sizes. "The Chinese may not be supposed to be distinguishing on the propriety of our figure, in these ill-suited uniforms; but we certainly appeared in a very strong point of ridicule to each other."

On Monday, September 2, 1793, Macartney's convoy set off for Jehol at 1am in the morning. Even at this early hour, the road was blocked with curious Chinese onlookers, and it took six hours for the entourage to to get to the city gates. Their journey north took seven days, and was broken up with stops at the Imperial rest lodges along the way, a great honor for the party. Anderson studied the scenery carefully, noting that as they moved north, it became increasingly infertile. He was astounded to find that, despite the harsh conditions, even the tiniest arable plots of land in this desert were under cultivation. The highlight of this journey to Jehol was the moment when they passed through the Great Wall, "of which we had all heard or read with wonder and astonishment, which so few Europeans had ever seen, and which no one of our own country would probably ever see but ourselves: this was the great wall, the ancient boundary of China and Tartary, through whose portals our passage lay."

Anderson acknowledges the astonishing scale of the structure, saying: "This Wall, is, perhaps the most stupendous work ever produced by man; the length of it is supposed to be upwards of twelve hundred miles, and its height in the place where I stood upon it, for it varies in its circumstances, according to the nature of the surface, is upwards of thirty feet, and it is about twenty-four feet broad." Its grandeur, he concluded, "is not easily grasped by the strongest imagination."

But he confessed that the structure "did not altogether satisfy my expectations." He especially lamented signs of its decay. "But the most stupendous works of man must at length moulder away; and since Tartary and China are become one nation, and, consequently, subject to the same government, the wall has lost its importance...so that the time is approaching when this stupendous monument of persevering labour, when this unparalleled effort of national policy, will become an enormous length of ruins and an awful example of decay."

Several days after passing the Great Wall, the party arrived on September 8, dusty and bedraggled, at Chengde, the site of the imperial hunting grounds to which the Qing emperor repaired each autumn. They were taken to their quarters to clean themselves and lined up in formation for their grand entrance, but this was not done to Anderson's exacting standards and again he complained:

"There was indeed somewhat of a parade in all this business, but it was by no means calculated to impress a favourable idea of the greatness of the British nation, on the minds of those who beheld it: they might be pleased with its novelty, but it did not, in any degree, possess that characteristic appearance which was so necessary on this occasion. The military departments made a respectable figure, and the gentlemen of the suite cannot be supposed for one moment to derogate from the diplomatic character in which they were involved; but the rest of the company exhibited a very awkward appearance: some wore round hats, some cocked hats, and others straw hats; some were in whole boots, some in half boots, and others in shoes with colored stockings. In short, unless it was in second hand coats and waistcoats, which did not fit them, the inferior part of the suite did not even enjoy the appearance of shabby uniformity."

He was little surprised then, when later that day Macartney was snubbed by the Imperial Minister of State. He went on to list the many subsequent slights encountered by the Embassy at Chengde (insufficient food, being ignored by important figures, severe delays in visiting the Emperor), stating that it was the disordered appearance of the suite that had lead to such poor behaviour on the part of the Chinese. Anderson supported his argument with an anecdote: at one point, Macartney was visited by a mandarin of some stature.

"During the visit of the mandarin, his attendants were very busily employed in examining the dress of the English servants; the lace of which they rubbed with a stone to certify its quality, and then looking at each other with an air of surprise, they shook their heads and smiled; a sufficient proof that the Tartars are not unacquainted with the value of metals; at least they clearly comprehended the inferior value of the trimmings that decorated the liveries of the embassy."

Shortly after this visit, the rations went downhill rapidly – obviously (in Anderson's eyes) the result of their sub-standard clothing.

A few days later, the invitation from the Emperor was finally issued to Macartney, and an early-morning escort was arranged to lead him to the palace. While Anderson expressed his pleasure with their seeming change in fortunes, he was shocked that no improvements had been made to the party's appearance, as this could only lead to further bad behavior on the part of the Chinese. While making its way through the dark streets of the Chengde in the pre-dawn light, the music of the escort drew animals of all shapes and sizes to the procession, and they soon found themselves tripping over dogs, pigs and donkeys in an undignified manner.

"After a confused cavalcade, if it can deserve that name, we arrived at the Palace of the Emperor, in the same state of confusion in which we had proceeded... In short, it appeared to the greater part of those who were concerned in it, to be rather ridiculous to attempt to make a parade that no one could see."

Anderson predicted failure for this meeting, but Macartney

and Staunton returned to their quarters in high spirits. The Emperor, it seemed, "was singularly impressed by young Master Staunton", Staunton's twelve-year-old son George, who could speak and write some Chinese. The Emperor had gone so far as to give Master Staunton a personal gift. This was taken as a very positive sign, and, several hours later, carts full of presents from the Emperor were delivered to the party. Another meeting (followed by even more gifts) was declared a further success as well.

"The evening of this day was passed in great mirth and festivity by the whole suite, from the very favourable forebodings which they now entertained of the final success of their important mission," reported Anderson.

The entire party was then invited to attend the birthday celebrations for the Emperor at his palace. All were dressed in their "finery" and traveled directly into the personal gardens of the Emperor, where, Anderson said, they were graced with the honor of all honors, an opportunity to glimpse the Emperor.

"This great personage was in a very plain palanquin borne by 20 mandarins of the first order; and were it not for that circumstance, he could not have been distinguished from a common mandarin, as he wore no mark or badge of distinction, nor any article of dress superior to the higher classes of his subjects. The simplicity of his appearance, it seems, proceeds from that wise policy which distinguishes his reign, as it is a principle of his government to check, as much as possible, all useless luxury."

With the Embassy going smoothly, it was decided that the British would wrap up their stay in Jehol – Macartney apparently having received enough positive signals that they would "get down to business" back in Peking.

This optimism was overshadowed by an event that left

Anderson enraged as he considered the potentially lethal damage done to the Embassy's image. Engaging in any trade with the Chinese was expressly forbidden for members of the Embassy, but before disembarking Macartney had informed the entire party that they would be living under martial law while in China and any deviance from the rules would be immediately punished by a military tribunal. So when a British soldier was caught trading knick-knacks for Chinese wine in Jehol, he was duly court-martialed and sentenced to sixty lashes.

"Such an idea, as might be supposed, occasioned no small abhorrence as well as alarm in the minds of those who would be affected by a regulation so contrary to every principle of right or justice", but Anderson found it even more reprehensible that the punishment of this soldier was exacted before their Chinese hosts. The British believed that their Chinese handlers would be pleased to see them so strictly enforcing their trade policies, but their violent display, according to Anderson, was deemed ill-mannered and repulsive.

"Whether this punishment was necessary to the discipline or good orders of the troops, I do not profess to consider, but of this I am sure, that it was by no means necessary to make it a public spectacle, and to risque the unfavourable impressions which it might, and indeed did, make in the minds of the Chinese, before whom it was purposely exhibited."

The Embassy members seemed in good spirits, convinced that their mission would be met with success. But Anderson noted that they when one of their party passed away en route, they held a secret burial so as not to worry the Emperor that the British had carried disease into the country.

Back in the capital, Macartney ordered his team to get to work converting their assigned quarters into his permanent residence. The "State Canopy" was set up, large portraits of the British monarch painted and hung, a hospital arranged, and furniture and dishes unpacked. Macartney spent his days penning letters for the fleet's captain to carry back to England, because, "it was then being considered by Lord Macartney as a settled arrangement with the court of Pekin that the English embassy should remain in that city during the winter, to carry on the important negotiations with which it was entrusted."

Just as domestic arrangements were getting into full swing, the Emperor arrived back in the city and Macartney was granted an audience to present the British Embassy's demands. Anderson accompanied Macartney to the Emperor's palace, but was required to stay in the forecourt of the "Forbidden City", which he found disappointing.

"Though I am ready to acknowledge that the palace had something imposing in its appearance, when compared with the diminutive buildings of the city that surround it, I could see nothing that disposed me to believe the extraordinary accounts I had heard and read of the wonders of the Imperial residence of Pekin."

After returning from the audience with the Emperor, Macartney redoubled his orders for domestic arrangements to be completed, leaving the entire party, Anderson included, convinced that the mission had been a complete success.

This blithe optimism was short-lived. On October 6, 1793, Macartney feigned illness after arriving at the Palace for a meeting with the Emperor and by the afternoon of that day, Anderson reported that there was rampant gossip in the servants' quarters about an imminent departure. The next morning, Macartney made a formal announcement that the entire party was to quit Peking in two days' time.

Anderson was not especially shocked by the news, as after the "ugly uniform" affair, he had never been particularly optimistic.

He was, however, taken aback by the short amount of time given for packing, especially as Macartney and Staunton had been encouraging unpacking up to that point. As a valet, Anderson found this quick deadline decidedly unfair, particularly as he was then asked to make arrangements so that "the Ambassador might not appear to be turned out of the metropolis of a country, where he had represented the crown of Great Britain."

Inspired by the protests of his staff, Macartney requested a few days' extension from the Chinese authorities. This was agreed, and then retracted. In a similarly frustrating diplomatic turn of affairs, realizing his carriage could not be dismantled in time, Macartney tried to give it to the Imperial Minister of State, who wrote back refusing it – yet did not return the carriage.

Though earlier packing arrangements had impressed Anderson with their efficiency, this one was, by contrast, an absolute mess. Most of the packing cases had already been converted to furniture and fixtures in the proceeding weeks, meaning the villa needed to be literally ripped apart to pull together all of their belongings. Many valuable items were given away because there was no time to pack them. The "Royal Canopy" was torn from the walls and the silk shreds distributed to the Chinese servants. The items that were to be taken were then jammed into carts, many not in packing cases. This hasty, disorderly departure was further complicated when one of the soldiers died during the packing. Still not wishing to provoke suspicions about British diseases, valuable time and resources were used to make sure his body was "spirited away" unseen. The Embassy finally left the city in the early hours of October 9 and with Anderson bitterly commenting:

"In short, we entered Pekin like paupers; we remained in it like prisoners; and we quitted it like vagrants."

The Embassy left Peking with none of the fanfare that had

greeted their arrival. Where once they had been housed in private villas, they now found themselves confined to haylofts, and the food quality had tapered off accordingly. When they reached the place where the party was to transfer to a fleet of junks, they found only a muddy bank for dumping the luggage.

"In short, those attentions which were shown to the Ambassador on his former abode in this city, seemed to have been forgotten, and the place which was now appropriated to receive the baggage was a small spot on the side of the river, and protected only by a screen of matting."

Anderson noted with wonder that the carriage that had earlier been spurned by the Imperial Minister of State had reappeared, looking much the worse for wear.

Once the Embassy was aboard the junks conditions improved. Anderson found the trip on cabals through China – from Peking in the north to Canton in the south – to be a highlight of the journey. The Embassy was given the honor of traveling south via the Grand Canal, something no previous Western party had done. Military detachments had been ordered to guard the banks of the canal as the Embassy passed. Whether they were there to honor the Embassy or keep it in isolation was unclear, but Anderson was pleased by the gesture.

"There could be no reason to suppose that the Emperor had not even been anxious to render our departure from his kingdom as agreeable as respect and exterior honour could make it. In short from Tartary to Canton, it was a chain of salutes which were so frequent, as I have before observed, that it might be compared almost to a train of wild fire laid from one end of the empire to the other."

Speculation about the Embassy's rapid departure was rife on the return trip:

"In the very unexpected situation of the embassy, it was very natural for those who composed the retinue of it to be continually forming conjectures, and eagerly inquiring after any information that might tend to elucidate the extraordinary circumstances of it."

Anderson rejected one particular theory: that an evil mandarin had badmouthed the British to the Emperor, saying that they were "barbarous, inhuman and destitute of all those amiable qualities which they pretended to possess."

It was on this trip down the canals that Anderson was able to get his closest look at China. His insights were far-ranging: he commented on everything from the smoking habits of children ("Children, as soon as they have sufficient strength or dexterity to hold a pipe in their hands, are taught by their parents to smoke, which they feel not only as an habitual amusement, but is considered a preservative against all contagious diseases") to the postal system (superior to that in England) and cormorant fishing ("most extraordinary!").

He found the scenery stunning, and he was particularly impressed by the towering red pagodas. As the trip down the canals lasted over two months and there was little to do besides watch the countryside scroll by, boredom gradually set in. Anderson continued to note his observations, but had seen so much scenery that he lost track of where they were and started making up names for the towns they passed.

"Though this country abounds in a succession of never ceasing variety to the traveller, it will not, I fear, possess that pleasing appearance in the opinion of the reader; as it is impossible to convey, by words, that diversifying character to the page of a printed book, which is seen in every leaf of the volume of Nature...Thus, I fear, it will prove, that while the writer is receiving pleasure from the variety of objects that occur to his memory, he is preparing dullness for the reader by an enumeration of them."

From this point, he resolved to share only his most thrilling anecdotes, and his reports grew less frequent. On December 7, he quipped: "This was the most extraordinary day which we had yet known in China, as we saw neither city, town or village in the course of it."

Finally, on December 18, 1793, the British Embassy's fleet of junks reached the end of their journey through China as they arrived in Canton. They were at least released from the custody of their Chinese handlers (Anderson was sad to bid adieu to Van-Tadge-In) and were allowed to move into the British East India Company's factory quarters on Shameen Island.

Anderson noted with relief that the homesick Embassy was able to again partake "of the habitual comforts of our native soil" and even celebrate Christmas. No longer under armed guard, he took long strolls through the city and was particularly struck by the cosmopolitan factory district, where flags from around the world could be seen flying.

He was also surprised by the shops he encountered. "[The shops] are fitted up within after the English manner, to which the inhabitants appear to have a decided partiality. Indeed, it was not uncommon to see their names written on the signs in English characters and adapted to English orthography."

His positive impressions were tempered by the character of the Hong merchants who traded with the Westerners, and the Cantonese in general – he found them to be "knavish in the extreme" – and he said he believed that it was contact with Europeans that had caused this behaviour.

After selling their brass band to the East India Company to help keep up morale among the British expatriots, the Embassy moved on to Macao and then, at last, headed home. By this point, Anderson was exhausted, with his narrative trailing off to nothing more than a few paragraphs. He politely excused himself thus: "It would be not only superfluous, but impertinent in me, to add another description to the many which have already been given [of Canton and Macao]."

The homeward journey was smooth sailing most of the way, aside from pesky Malay pirates around Sumatra, and on September 3, 1794, six months after they had departed, Anderson and the rest of the Embassy gratefully reached home, disappointed and somewhat the worse for wear, but still in high spirits.

"At 5:00pm, we anchored safe, after a long and curious voyage, at Spithead; and soon felt the inexpressible satisfaction of once more treading the terra firma of our native country."

2

ÉVARISTE RÉGIS HUC

A JOURNEY THROUGH THE CHINESE EMPIRE

EVARISTE REGIS HUC WAS a French Roman Catholic missionary born in 1812, who had some extraordinary adventures, traveling about China and Central Asia in the 1840s and 1850s, when most of that part of the world had yet to be visited by a white man. He was deeply religious, and fanatically devoted to the work of spreading the Good Word amongst the Chinese pagans. But even though he spoke Chinese, his contempt for his would-be flock sometimes overflowed, especially when discussing their ungratefulness at not welcoming the Roman Catholic faith en masse with open arms.

Huc was sent by the Vincentian order to Macao in 1839, and for the next five years lived and worked in a number of places in both southern and northern China. In 1844, he set out from To-lun, a town north of Peking, and then traveled to Tibet with a fellow French missionary, Joseph Gabet. They reached Lhasa in January 1846 and were welcomed by the Tibetans. But the Imperial Chinese representative in Lhasa had Huc and Gabet expelled from Tibet. His exploits on this trip to Tibet are recounted in his book Travels to Tartary and Thibet.

His book A Journey through the Chinese Empire takes up the story as Huc and Gabet are escorted eastwards from Tibet into China. As the English translator puts it in his introduction, much of the book is taken up with an account of "the curious game carried on between the eternal shuffling trickeries of the Mandarins, and the courage, humour and audacity of the missionaries." And Huc's account really is one of the classics of cultural arrogance.

The progress of Huc and Gabet out of Tibet and through China was in marked contrast to their secret journey from Macao up to northern China, and from there west to Tibet. They were now traveling openly in the company of mandarins, being escorted first to Chengdu, capital of Sichuan province, where their fate would be decided.

The first town they came into after leaving Tibet was called Ta-tsien-lou, surely today's Kangding, around 320 kilometers to the west of Chengdu, in the mountains above the plain. Huc decided a show of strength was necessary to let these border mandarins know who was in charge. "There was no middle course, we must either submit to their will or make them submit to ours."

The head mandarin in Ta-tsien-lou started out by forbidding the two missionaries to continue from continuing the journey in palanquins, the litters carried usually by four men, but Huc declares: "He was obliged to give way, however, thanks to the energy and perseverance of our protests."

There was also the question of what Huc and Gabet should wear for the journey. They decided to abandon their Tibetan furs, smelling strongly of mutton and yak butter, and had some Chinese gowns made, complete with red sashes and embroidered yellow caps. The authorities were outraged at this, as the red sash and yellow cap were supposed to be worn only by members of the Imperial family. But Huc insisted, saying that as strangers they were not bound to follow the conventions of the Chinese empire. "Our obstinacy was not to be overcome – and the mandarins submitted – as they ought to do."

They started out along the high road between Tibet and Chengdu, passing long lines of coolies transporting brick tea from inland China towards Tibet.

"As our palanquin approached, they lifted up their heads and cast on us a furtive and painfully stupid look. And this, said we sadly, is what civilization, when corrupt and without religious faith, is able to make of man created in the image of God."

They dropped out of the mountains and entered the heavily-populated areas of Sichuan province, and as they passed along the increasingly broad roads bordered by well-tended fields and ever-more numerous villages, the locals flocked out to gaze in astonishment on the two men from the Western Seas.

"The peasants abandoned their field labors, to run and post themselves on the road side to see us pass by. At the entrance of the towns, especially, the curious came thronging about us in such numbers that the palanquins could scarcely make their way through the throng. Our bearers vociferated, the soldiers who formed our escort tried to disperse them by dealing out blows right and left with their rattans, and while we advanced, as through the midst of an insurrection, all those thousands of little Chinese eyes were peering into our palanquins with the most eager curiosity. Loud remarks were made, without the smallest ceremony, on the cut of our physiognomies, our beards, noses, eyes, costume – nothing was forgotten. Some appeared pretty well satisfied with us, but others burst into shouts of laughter, as soon as they caught sight of what seemed to them our burlesque European features. A magic effect was, however, produced by the yellow cap and red sash. Those who first discovered them, pointed them out to their neighbors with evident amazement, and their faces immediately assumed a grave and severe expression. Some said that the Emperor had charged us with an extraordinary mission, and that he had himself bestowed on us these Imperial decorations. Others were of opinion that we were European spies who had been arrested in Thibet, and that we were to be tried as a preparatory ceremony to that of having our heads cut off. These various opinions which we heard expressed all around us, were sometimes amusing, but most frequently, it must be owned, vexatious."

At the town of Ya-tcheou, today's Ya'an, about 130 kilometers to the southeast of Chengdu, the natives became even more aroused by the presence of white men, and crowded into the inn in which Huc and his party were staying, clamoring for a view of the Europeans.

"The matter was now becoming serious, and it was evidently important to let them see who was master. By a sudden inspiration we seized a long and thick bamboo, which happened to be lying near the door of the room, and the poor Chinese, imagining no doubt that we intended to knock them down with it, tumbled over each other in their haste to get away. We then ran to the door of the room occupied by our Mandarin conductor, who, not knowing what to do in the riot, had bethought himself of the safe expedient of hiding himself. But as soon as we had found him, without giving him time to speak, or even to think, we seized him by the arm, clapped on his head his official hat, and dragged him along as fast as we could run to the gate of the inn. Then we thrust into his hands the great bamboo with which we had armed ourselves, and enjoined him to stand sentinel. "If," said we, "a single individual passes that gate, you are a lost man;" and hearing us talk in this grand style, the poor man took it seriously and did not dare to stir. The people in the street burst out laughing, for it was something new to see a military Mandarin mounting guard with a long bamboo perfectly quiet up to the time of our going to bed, the guard was then relieved, and our warrior laid down his arms and returned to his room, to console himself by smoking some pipes of tobacco. Those who do not know the Chinese, will doubtless be scandalized at our behavior, and will blame us severely. They will ask, what right we had to make this Mandarin ridiculous and expose him to the laughter of the people. The right, we answer, that every man had to provide for his personal safety."

Furthermore, Huc found out that their mandarin guides were cheating them by lodging them in cheap inns and pocketing most of the amount provided for their accommodation and food.

They stopped for afternoon tea at a large Buddhist monastery. Huc said the monks there were full of courtesy, "but we could not discover many signs of faith or devotion in their skeptical and cunning faces".

Twelve days after leaving the border town of Ta-tsien-lou, they arrived in Chengdu, capital of Sichuan Province. As they approached the city walls, a detail of soldiers appeared to escort them through the crowded streets.

"Our hearts beat somewhat quicker than usual, for we knew that we were about to be brought to trial by order of the Emperor. Were we to be sent to Pekin, to Canton, or to another world. There had been nothing to alarm us hitherto, but in the absolute uncertainty of what we had to expect, it was pardonable that we should experience a little emotion."

Huc was impressed by Chengdu, especially after the primitive hardships of the Tibetan plateau.

"The principal streets are of a good width, paved entirely with large flagstones, and so clean that you can scarcely, as you pass through them, believe yourself to be in a Chinese town."

They were taken to a tribunal, where they impressed the local mandarin by being able to read a wall inscription in the Manchu script. They were lodged in another tribunal, and the next morning received an invitation to dinner from the local prefect. The two missionaries were joined by two mandarins who discreetly attempted to pump Huc and his colleague for information about where they had been and what they had been doing. They had fun dodging the mandarins' questions. When tea was served at the end of the meal, one of the mandarins went out and came back with a bible and a crucifix, which he said a Christian had given him as a present.

Huc opened the Bible and found inside the name of a French missionary who had been put to death in Chengdu in 1815 after having been condemned in the tribunal where the dinner was being held. The mandarins, when told this, seemed astonished, and told Huc that whoever had told him this "fable" must have been joking.

Four days after their arrival in Chengdu, the two missionaries were informed that they were to be brought to trial.

"This news, as may well be supposed, was to us matter of great interest. A trial in China, and by order of the Emperor, was no trifle. Many of our now happy predecessors had only entered the tribunals to be tortured, and left them to suffer glorious martyrdom."

They were escorted to the tribunal, which they found surrounded by a huge crowd.

"The Mandarins who were to take part in the ceremonial arrived in succession, followed by suites of attendants, who had uncommonly the appearance of gangs of thieves. The satellites ran backward and forward, in their long red robes, and hideous peaked hats of black felt or iron wire, surmounted by long pheasant's feathers. They were armed with long rusty swords, and carried chains, pincers, and various instruments of torture, of strong and terrible forms."

Huc assumed the idea was to try and frighten them.

"At length every one had found his place, and the tumult was succeeded by a profound silence. A moment afterward a terrible cry, uttered by a great number of voices, was heard in the hall of audience, it was repeated three times, and our companions told us that it was on the judges making their solemn entry and installing themselves in their seats. Two officers, decorated with the Crystal Ball, then appeared, and made us a sign to follow them. They came between us, our companions placed themselves behind, and the two accused persons walked thus to judgement.

"A great door was then suddenly opened, and we beheld, at a glance, the numerous personages of this Chinese performance. Twelve stone steps led up to the vast inclosure where the judges were placed, on each side of this staircase was a line of executioners in red dresses, and when the accused passed tranquilly through their ranks, they all cried out with a loud voice, "Tremble! Tremble!" and rattled their instruments of torture. We were stopped at about the middle of the hall, and then eight officers of the court proclaimed in a chanting voice the customary formula: "Accused! on your knees! on your knees! The accused remained silent and motionless. The summons was repeated, but there was still no alteration in their attitude. The two officers with the Crystal Ball, now thought themselves called on to come to our assistance, and pulled our arms to help us to kneel down. But a solemn look and some few emphatic words sufficed to make them let go their hold. They even judged it expedient to retire a little, and kept a respectful distance."

Huc informed the judges: "Every empire has its own customs and manners."

The judges decided to ignore the lack of manners shown by the French missionaries and the Inspector of Crimes, "a wrinkled old man with a face like a polecat", began the interrogation.

"He discoursed with great volubility concerning the majesty

of the Celestial Empire, and the inviolability of its territory, reproached us with our Audacity, with our vagabondizing life about the provinces and among the tributary nations, and then fired off at us a volley of questions, which certainly proved his eager desire to become acquainted with every particular concerning us. He asked who had introduced us to the Empire, with whom we had entered into any relation, whether there were many European missionaries in China, where they lived, what resources they could command for their subsistence, and finally, a crowd of questions that appeared to us exceedingly impertinent. His tone and manner, too, were by no means in accordance with politeness and "the rites;" and it became necessary to give this man a lesson, and moderate his impetuosity. While he was perorating at a great rate, and allowing his eloquence to overflow into all sorts of subjects, we listened to him with great calmness and patience. When he had finished, we said to him: "We men of the West, you see, like to discuss matters of business with coolness and method, but your language had been so diffuse and violent, that we have scarcely been able to make out your meaning. Be so good as to begin again, and express your thoughts more clearly and more peaceably."

The Inspector of Crimes spluttered angrily at this slight, and the president of the court took up the questioning, asking who had brought them to China and with whom they had lodged. Huc replied that, sadly, they could not answer.

Another court official then gave them a sheet of paper on which were crudely written the letters of the European alphabet, and told Huc to read them out.

"One of us had the complaisance to speak solemnly his A B C, and during the time, each of the judges drew from his boot, which in China often serves for a pocket, a copy of the alphabet, in which the pronunciation of every European letter had been given, better or worse, in Chinese characters. It seems that this incident had been concerted and prepared beforehand. Every judge had his eyes intently fixed upon the paper, and doubtless promised himself to make in this one lesson great progress in a European language. The Assessor of the Left, keeping his eyes and the forefinger of his right hand fixed on the first letter, and addressing himself to the one of the prisoners who had just said A B C, begged him to repeat the letters slowly, and pause a little on each. The prisoner, however, making four steps forward, and politely extending his alphabet toward the philological judge, observed: "I had thought we came here to submit to trial, but it seems we came to be schoolmasters, and you to be our scholars.'"

The tribunal members shook with laughter. The president enquired as to why the French bothered to send people to make Christians in China, and asked for some information on the Christian religion, which Huc eagerly gave. Finally, the president called for an adjournment and two days later, the missionaries were informed that there would be no need of a second judicial examination, and that they were to be summoned before the provincial viceroy to be told what had been decided regarding their fates.

They were transported to the mansion of the Manchu viceroy Pao-hing, a cousin of the Emperor himself, in two sumptuous state palanquins and then ushered into Pao-hing's presence. After some polite conversation, the viceroy asked the two missionaries to stand beside him.

"He set himself to take a deliberate survey of our personal appearance first of one and then of the other, while he at the same time amused himself by turning in his mouth fragments of the Areca nut, which the Mantchous like so much to chew. He took several pinches of snuff also, out of a little phial, and had the courtesy to offer it to us, though without speaking, and still seeming as profoundly occupied with observing our features as if he were about to take our portraits. We considered that he admired our beauty, for he asked whether we had any medicine or recipe for preserving that fresh and florid complexion. We replied that the temperament of Europeans differed much from that of the Chinese, but that in all countries a sober and well regulated course of life was the best means of preserving health."

The viceroy asked them where they wanted to go, and the missionaries said they wanted to return to Tibet. The viceroy rejected this idea immediately, saying: "Thibet is a good-for-nothing place", and adding: "Now that you are here, I must send you to Canton."

"Since we are not free, send us where you please," replied Huc.

The viceroy decreed that Huc and Gabet could rest in Chengdu for a while and would then be escorted to Canton, the port in southern China which at that time was still virtually the only place in China where foreigners were allowed to go, in spite of the Opium War a few years earlier and the treaty Britain had forced China to sign, opening other ports to foreigners and foreign trade.

After 15 days in Chengdu, Huc was "beginning to get exceedingly tired of the city", so he let the viceroy know that they were anxious to start their journey, and it was decided that they should leave in two days' time. They were immediately inundated with requests from various mandarins to be allowed to be their escort to Wuchang, the capital of Hubei province to the east.

"All these candidates were, if you could take their word for it, absolutely perfect men."

They explained to Huc how they were experienced, possessed the "five cardinal virtues", and knew the country to be traversed well.

"What all these fine things really meant," said Huc, "was that there was a little fortune to be gained by him who should have the chance to escort us. According to the benevolent intentions of the viceroy, we were to travel like government officers of rank. In that case extraordinary contributions would be levied on all the countries through which we passed, to provide for our expenses and those of our escort, and the gentlemen who desired so greatly to be our conductors thought to profit by our inexperience in such matters, and retain for their own share the greater part of the funds that would be allotted for the purpose by the tribunals on our road. There exist every minute regulations concerning these sorts of journeys, but they thought we should know nothing about them. We took very good care, however, not to choose our conductors ourselves, we preferred leaving the appointment to the superior authorities, reserving in this manner the right of complaining if things did not afterward turn out to our satisfaction."

Two mandarins were chosen for them, one a literary scholar named Ting, a man "of the middle size, very thin, marked with the small-pox and worn out with the use of opium; a great talker and exceedingly ignorant." The other was a young military officer, an opium addict like Ting, but "more polished and courteous".

Inspired by these two, Huc discoursed at length on the evils of the god-less Chinese government and society, but adds: "We must not wholly despise the Chinese, there may be even much that is admirable and instructive in their ancient and curious institutions."

But when discussing the apparent reluctance of the Chinese people to embrace the one true faith, Roman Catholicism, Huc's anger and frustration spills over:

"Truly lamentable is this obstinacy of the Chinese people in rejecting, disdainfully, the treasure of faith, that Europe has never ceased to offer with so much zeal, devotion, and perseverance. No other nation has excited such lively solicitude on the part of the church, no sacrifice has been spared for its sake, and yet it is the one, of all, that has proved most rebellious. The soil has been prepared and turned in all directions with patience and intelligence, it has been watered by sweat and tears, and enriched with the blood of martyrs, the evangelical seed has been sown in it with profusion, the Christian world has poured forth prayers, to draw upon it the blessing of Heaven, and yet it is still as sterile as ever, and the time of the harvest is not yet come."

He laments the failure of previous attempts to introduce Christianity to China, both by the Nestorian Christians more than a thousand years ago, and by the Jesuits in the 16th and 17th centuries.

"Religious ideas, do not, it must be owned, strike very deep root in this country," says Huc. "A melancholy trait is it in the character of this people, that Christian truth does but glide over its surface!"

Again and again, he says, China had disappointed the Church, and converts seemed reluctant to die for their faith as proud marytrs, inexplicably preferring to renounce their faith in the face of official persecution. But "the Church is never discouraged. The moment circumstances appeared in the slightest degree more favorable, Evangelical labourers presented themselves, no less zealous and devoted than their predecessors."

Huc says the propagation of the Gospel was not going well. Jesuits no longer had a place in court, and Catholic priests had to slip into the country in secret and lived in fear of being discovered by the authorities. The work of recruiting and training local priests was desperately slow, but had to be continued if Roman Catholicism was to one day save the whole Empire.

"It is they who can act most directly on the infidels, instruct them in the truths of religion, and exhort them to renounce the superstitions of Buddhism. But unfortunately, their zeal for the conversion of their brethren is seldom very ardent, and they need to be constantly kept up to the mark by all kinds of encouragements."

He estimated that at the time of writing – the late 1850s – there were perhaps 800,000 Christians in the Chinese empire, out of a total population of maybe 300 million.

"Such an amount of success is not, it must be owned, very encouraging when it is remembered that it is the result of many centuries of preaching, and of the efforts of countless missionaries. It is natural that our readers should ask what may be considered the cause of this deplorable sterility. First, then, it is indisputable that, as the Government is opposed to Christianity, the timid and pusillanimous Chinese will have no great inclination to profess it, to brave the hostility of the mandarins, and defying persecution, to exclaim with pious daring, "It is better to disobey man that God!" They will excuse themselves by referring to the prohibition of the Emperor."

Huc defends the Church and its missionaries from the charge that they are the vanguard of European imperialism, although he admits that with European nations busily establishing colonies in all parts of the Orient, the Chinese authorities could be forgiven for their suspicions.

"The Chinese, therefore, are thoroughly convinced that, under pretense of religion, we are really manœuvring for the invasion of the Empire, and the overthrow of the dynasty, and it must be owned, that they have under their eyes certain facts that have no tendency to convince them of their mistake."

The Chinese government was continuing with its persecution of Chinese Christians in the belief that all Christians were in reality spies for the European powers, but Huc adds that the real reason for the Church's lack of success lay elsewhere, in the Chinaman's lack of religious conviction.

"It is this radical, profound indifference to all religion – an indifference that is scarcely conceivable by any who have not witnessed it – which is in our opinion the real, grand obstacle that has so long opposed the progress of Christianity in China. The Chinese is so completely absorbed in temporal interests, in the things that fall under his senses, that his whole life is only materialism put in action. Lucre is the sole object on which his eyes are constantly fixed. A burning thirst to realize some profit, great or small, absorbs all his faculties – the whole energy of his being. He never pursues any thing with ardor but riches and material enjoyments. God – the soul – a future life – he believes in none of them, or, rather, he never thinks about them at all. If he ever takes up a moral or religious book, it is only by way of amusement – to pass the time away. It is a less serious occupation than smoking a pipe, or drinking a cup of tea."

After this aside on the dire state of Christianity in China, Huc picks up his narrative again as they are leaving Chengdu on their way eastwards.

"After a three hours' march, we reached a Koung-kouan, or communal palace, where we were to rest for a little while and take some refreshments." On the orders of the provincial Viceroy, the local mandarins had prepared iced lemonade for them – the Viceroy had found out that Europeans disapproved of the Chinese habit of drinking hot tea during the summer, and preferred cool drinks. Huc once more praises the Manchu Viceroy, and adds that "in general, we have met with much more devotion of characters among the Manchus than the Chinese – always more generosity and less treachery."

The very first day of their march, they had problems with

Master Ting, their chief escort. The comfortable palanquins they had been shown before the start of the journey had been replaced by cheaper models, "narrow travelling prisons", while each palanquin was carried by only three bearers instead of the expected four – Ting was of course pocketing the difference.

"We were not surprised at this, for we knew that a Chinese can scarcely ever keep the straight path of himself, but has to be forcefully brought back to it. We did not, however, expect to have to begin the very first day, and it did not seem a good augury."

Huc confronted Ting about the palanquin-switch, and Ting assured them that transport more befitting their exalted station would be available in the next town, which they would reach the following day.

The next morning, they arrived at a town on the banks of the Yangtze River, and Ting informed them that they were to proceed for a way by water. The prospect of a boat ride pleased the missionaries, and they immediately boarded the junk provided. Once everything, including the palanquins, was on board, the members of the Chinese escort settled themselves down in various parts of the boat.

"It has always seemed to us, that the nature of a Chinese, body and soul, had an astonishing resemblance to that of India-rubber. The suppleness of their minds can only be compared to the elasticity of their corporeal frames, and it is worth seeing how, when they have found a snug corner, be it ever so small, they will manage to stuff themselves in, and curl themselves round, and make a perfect nest of it, and when they have once taken up such a position, they are settled in it for the day."

Ting and the military officer settled themselves in a little curtained alcove and began smoking opium. After a few pipes, Ting especially seemed to be in "a state of the highest self-satisfaction", the cause of which, Huc says, was "the handsome profit he expected to make out of the journey."

"This trip on the water we found had only been undertaken in consequence of a little prudent calculation. At every stage, the Mandarin of the place where we stopped was obliged to supply all the wants of the party, as well as the expenses of the road to the next stage, and to furnish bearers for the palanquins, and horses for the soldiers. These corvées cost considerable sums. Now Master Ting had made his little arrangements thus: he sent forward his scribe along the route we were to have followed, to gather the appointed tribute, but graciously to inform the Mandarins that he would spare them all the trouble of the affair by proceeding by water. It was easy, as we were going down the river, to do in one day the distance of four stages, and as the hiring of a boat costs very little, the profits became enormous."

Some time after midnight, they arrived at a town called Kientcheou, where they were lodged at the Hotel of Accomplished Wishes. Huc was unhappy that they had not been taken to the town's communal palace – the official guest house – and he was even more displeased when Mandarin Ting woke them at the crack of dawn the next day to tell them to prepare to set off again.

"'Take yourself off, Master Ting,' said we, 'as quickly as you can – and moreover, if anyone else has the impudence to come disturbing us, we will get you degraded.'"

Huc insisted that new palanquins be found. Ting and the local mandarins insisted that there were no palanquins in the town, and that the finest palanquins were only available at Tchoung-tching (Chungking).

"In that case, then," said Huc, "find a man who understands these things and send him directly to Tchoung-tching to get some palanquins. We will wait here."

Huc then returned to his room.

The mandarins were horrified by this – it meant the French

missionaries would be staying in the town for who knew how long. They sent delegations to see Huc and to try to get him to change his mind.

"They invented the most absurd tales, they heaped lie upon lie to prove to us that we must set out immediately. But to all this we had but one answer: 'When men like us take a resolution, it is irrevocable.' "

Finally, the mandarins came up with a pair of palanquins, which Huc examined and pronounced acceptable.

"Thereupon arose a new question. The Mandarins looked at one another, and asked, 'Who is to pay?'"

The Mandarins began arguing, so Huc suggested that Ting as their chief escort should bear the cost.

"The Mandarins of Kien-tcheou burst out laughing, and said our solution to the problem was capital. Master Ting was foaming with rage and uttering yells as if his inside was being torn out."

But Ting was forced to accept the ruling, and mournfully counted out the cash.

In an aside at this point, Huc describes something of Chinese cuisine. The Chinese have their faults, but one thing they are good at, he says, is cooking.

"If you want a cook, it is the easiest thing in the world to supply your want, you have but to take the first Chinese you can catch, and after a few days' practice he will acquit himself of his duties to admiration."

But he criticizes certain European writers who, he says, had had a joke at the European public's expense by reporting that the Chinese ate such weird dishes as shark's fins, fish-gizzards and goose-feet. Such reports were entirely untrue, says Huc, although he adds that it was possible that some Canton merchants had mischievously amused themselves at the expense of Europeans newly-arrived in China by "serving them up dishes invented expressly for them, and which had never before made their appearance at a Chinese table."

The joke here, however, is on Huc, because Chinese people, especially those in Canton, love eating shark's fins, fish-gizzards, goose-feet and a host of other unlikely dishes.

They set off again, along roads that became increasingly worse as they progressed. They passed through Chungking, where they added an extra military Mandarin their retinue, and one day stopped at a town called Leang-chan. Huc understood that Christians were numerous in the town, and he let it be known that he would welcome visits from the faithful. He was visited by a number of local Christians, and the Mandarins were very suspicious of these local people who seemed to be so intimate with the foreigners.

Just before nightfall, while Huc was strolling in the garden of the town's official guest house and the mandarin escorts were sitting under a tree smoking their pipes, "our servant crossed the garden with a letter and a small packet, and took the way toward our room. The military Mandarin whom we had taken at Tchoung-king immediately followed him, and though he had chosen his time well, we did nevertheless perceive his move, and ran to our room to see what the audacious spy was doing. We caught him in flagrante delicto reading our letter and rummaging in the parcel addressed to us. As soon as he saw us he tried to bolt, keeping possession of the parcel, but we barred his passage, drove him back into the room, shut the door, and sprang upon him, crying thieves! thieves! When he saw that we took hold of a rope as if to tie him, he cried out in his turn for help, and all the inmates of the palace in a moment came running to our room. We had no inclination to do any thing more than laugh at the adventure, but in China it was necessary to go into a violent passion, and accordingly we did so. The packet, which was open, contained only some dried fruits and perfumed necklaces, which a Christian family had the kindness to offer us."

Also inside the parcel was a letter signed by the head of the Tchao family.

The military mandarin, says Huc, trembled with fright. Just then, the town's prefect arrived and announced that the head of the Tchao family had been arrested for causing the disturbance.

"'A trial! A trial!' we exclaimed, 'we must have a trial!' If the head of the family of Tchao has committed any offense, let him be punished according to the laws for an example to the people. But if the head of that family is innocent, then it is the military Mandarin of Tchoung-king who is the guilty party, and he must be punished."

The local mandarins tried to calm Huc and offered to pardon Mr. Tchao. But Huc was not to be deflected from his course, and insisted that they would not leave Leang-chan until the trial had been held.

Finally, towards midnight, Huc was woken and informed that the mandarins were waiting to begin the trial. He rose and dressed in his finest clothes and went to the tribunal.

"We were introduced into the hall of audience, which was splendidly lit with large lanterns of variously coloured paper. A multitude of curious spectators, among whom were probably many Christians, thronged the lower end of the hall. The principal Mandarins of the town and our three conductors were seated at the upper part on a raised platform, where were several seats arranged before a long table. The judges gave us a most gracious reception, and the prefect begged us to be seated immediately, in order that they might commence proceedings. The question now arose, where were we to be seated? Nobody knew, and our presence appeared to create in the mind of the prefect himself some serious doubts on the subject of his prerogatives. He certainly bore an Imperial dragon, richly embroidered in relief on the front of his violet silk tunic, but then we had a dragon on a beautiful red girdle; the prefect had a blue ball, but then we had a yellow cap! After a few moments of hesitation we felt a sudden energetic inspiration to assume the direction of the affair ourselves, and, accordingly, we marched proudly up to the President's seat, and coolly motioned the others to the places they were to occupy, each according to his dignity. There was a moment of surprise, and even of hilarity among the Mandarins, but no opposition. They seemed so taken by surprise as to be completely put out, and mechanically assumed the places indicated."

The trial opened. Huc placed the main pieces of evidence – the little parcel and Tchao's letter – on the table before him. He asked the military Mandarin Lu if it was the parcel he had opened. Lu agreed that it was. The accused, Tchao, was brought in, and Huc asked him why he had sent the parcel.

"The humble Tchao family wished to express to the Spiritual Fathers the sentiments of their filial piety."

"How can that be?" replied Huc. "We do not know you, and you do not know us. We have never seen you."

"That is true, but those who are of the same religion are never strangers to one another, they make but one family, and when Christians meet, their hearts easily comprehend each other."

Huc turned to the Mandarins and asked them if the man had done anything wrong.

"All replied unanimously that his conduct was worthy of praise."

Huc pronounced Tchao to be not guilty and to be free to go, then added: "'It is evident that the conduct of the Mandarin Lu has been culpable, he introduced himself secretly into our apartment, and has covered his face with shame, by opening a letter that was addressed to us. The Mandarin Lu was appointed to be our military escort from the town of Tchoung-king to the frontiers of the province. But, as you see clearly that he has not received a good education, and his ignorance of the rites my lead him into still greater faults, we here declare that we will have nothing more to do with him: our declaration shall be made in writing, and sent to the superior authorities of Tchoung-king.' At these words we rose, and the sitting was over. Our admirable Christian came to us, threw himself on his knees, and asked our blessing."

Huc later wondered at the ease with which a French missionary had played the part of president of the court of a Chinese town, without any opposition.

"Two strangers, two barbarians, to be allowed to master for a moment all the rooted prejudices of a people jealous and disdainful of strangers to excess, and that even to the point of arrogating to themselves the authority of a judge, and exercising it officially! How could this be possible?"

His explanation was that the Imperial red girdle he was wearing had cast a powerful spell on the Chinese, noted for their respect for authority.

When they left Leang-chan the next morning, Huc noticed Mandarin Lu was no longer in their party, and they never saw him nor heard mention of him again.

They crossed from Sichuan province into Hubei, traveling sometimes by land, sometimes by river junk on their way to Wuchang, the provincial capital, now part of the huge industrial city of Wuhan sitting astride the Yangtze River. They passed through Yichang, a town on the Yangtze just below the famous gorges, after an unpleasant incident when one of the mandarins escorting them was found to be smuggling a large cargo of contraband salt in the hold of the missionaries' junk.

By Yichang itself, Huc was not impressed. He spent a day looking around the town, but "we found nothing remarkable in it...In general, all the great towns of China are much alike: there are crowds of people running about, and pushing against one another, but no public monuments, or anything to interest a traveller, such as he would find in Europe."

They stopped for the night at various towns along the way as their boat moved down the Yangtze, the river becoming wider each day until it was several miles across. The wind began to blow strongly, and the formerly calm river waters became increasingly rough.

"We went below, and found, as usual, our dear Mandarins lying side by side on mats, and smoking their accursed opium.

"During the whole morning the wind had been constantly increasing, and toward noon it came on to blow so violently, that we had to take in nearly all the sail, and keep only what was just necessary to steady the junk. The river was like a great arm of the sea lashed by a gale. The waves, though shorter and lower than in the open sea, were more impetuous, and dashed furiously against each other. Our poor junk rolling and pitching, at the same time groaned and creaked in every plank.

"While we were thus driven at the mercy of the winds and waves (but under the care of God), our Mandarins had taken refuge in a narrow cabin, where they cowered down without daring to move. We did not at all perceive on the faces of our two military gentlemen the haughty dignity that is proper to a soldier in a moment of danger. That Master Ting should want it was excusable: his quality of literary man gave him the right to be afraid. The fact was, all our conductors were affected by sea-sickness, and as they had never felt it before, nor even heard it mentioned, they all thought they were going to die."

Ting asked the missionaries for advice on his addiction to opium.

"Master Ting began to curse the day when he had allowed himself to yield to the temptation of this drug, and promised, that if he escaped with his life this time, he would throw pipe, lamp, and opium overboard. 'Why not do it now,' said we, 'what's the use of waiting?'

"'Oh, I am too ill now, I have not strength to move.'

"'Well, we are not at all ill, we can see to this little matter for you,' and we turned toward the place where he kept his smoking tools: but Master Ting was there before us. Suddenly awakened from his lethargy, he had made but one bound to the spot where his beloved casket was placed. The movement had been so nimble, and so totally unexpected, that his companions could not help laughing, though they were certainly not at all in the humour for it."

In the afternoon, they reached a bend in the river, and tried to round the point by tacking back and forth across the river. But the winds would not allow them to turn the point, and three times they were thrown upon the sandy river bank. On the third occasion, the master gave up and drove the junk deeper into the sandbank, in order to lessen the damage from the waves which angrily lashed the poorly-constructed boat. The sailors fastened the ship to trees on shore using strong cables, and they sat out the storm for a whole night. The next morning, the storm had abated, and the mandarins, particularly Master Ting, were surprised and pleased to find they were still alive.

"'Master Ting,' said we, 'You have escaped with your life and can move about quite well, so you must not forget to fulfill your promise: go and get your opium box, and let us pitch it overboard.' He only replied by cutting a caper, saying he had only said that in fun, and to show how little disposed he was to throw his pipe into the water, he went down and began to smoke with more ardor than ever."

On their arrival at a town called Kuen-kiang (Qianjiang), Huc was suddenly seized by violent vomiting and severe stomach pains. Chinese doctors were called but could do little to relieve the torment. The mandarins were frantic with anxiety – it would bode ill for them if this French missionary should die while in their charge. But four days later, the sickness passed, and the chief magistrate of the town visited Huc to say how concerned he had been at Huc's sickness – so concerned that he had gone so far as to choose a magnificent coffin for Huc at the finest coffin shop in town.

"Could there possibly be a more polite man? To have a coffin made quite ready for us in case we should want it – we could not fail to thank him with warmth for this most tender and delicate attention."

The next stop was the town of Tianmen where the local mandarins presented the missionaries with a pile of watermelons. Huc took the opportunity to describe the great Chinese love for eating watermelon seeds:

"We have always thought that the natural propensity of the Chinese for what is artificial and deceptive had inspired them with this frantic passion for water-melon seeds, for if there is in the world a disappointing dish, a fantastic kind of food it is this. Therefore the Chinese use them at all times and in all places."

The Chinese gnaw at these little seeds like rats, says Huc.

"The consumption of them throughout the empire is something incredible, something beyond the limits of the wildest imagination. You sometimes see junks on the rivers entirely loaded with this precious cargo, truly you might imagine yourself in a nation of rodentia."

They arrived at the city of Hanyang towards evening.

"The shop-keepers were already lighting their lanterns, and numerous groups of artisans who had finished their daily labor were on their way to the theatre, singing and frolicking as they went, while at the street corners spectators were gathered round jugglers and public readers. Every thing wore the lively, animated air of a densely-populated city, when, after the fatigues of a day of toil, all feel the necessity of a little rest and amusement."

But he adds that the Chinese are unaware of the pleasures of going for a stroll, taking an evening's constitutional.

"The public promenade is a thing unknown to the Chinese, who can not perceive either its charms or its wholesomeness. Those who have some notion of European manners think it very singular, if not utterly absurd, that we should find pleasure in walking for its own sake. When they hear that we consider it a refreshment and amusement, they regard us as very eccentric, or entirely devoid of common-sense. The Chinese of the interior whom business takes to Canton or Macao, always go the first thing to look at the Europeans on the promenade. It is one of the most amusing of sights for them. They squat in rows along the sides of the quays, smoking their pipes and fanning themselves, contemplating the while with a satirical and contemptuous eye the English and Americans who promenade up and down from one end to the other, keeping time with admirable precision.

"Europeans who go to China are apt to consider the inhabitants of the Celestial Empire very odd and supremely ridiculous, and the provincial Chinese at Canton and Macao pay back this sentiment with interest. It is very amusing to hear their sarcastic remarks on the appearance of the devils of the west, their utter astonishment at sight of their tight-fitting garments, their wonderful trowsers, and prodigious round hats, like chimney-pots – the shirt-collars adapted to cut off the ears, and making a frame around such grotesque faces, with long noses and blue eyes, no beard or mustache, but a handful of curly hair on each cheek. The shape of the dress-coat puzzles them above every thing. They try in vain to account for it, calling it a half garment, because it is impossible to make it meet over the breast, and because there is nothing in front to correspond to the tails behind. They admire the judgement and exquisite taste of putting buttons as big as sapecks behind the back where they never have any thing to button. How much handsomer they think themselves with their narrow, oblique, black eyes, high cheek bones, and little round noses, their shaven crowns and magnificent pigtails hanging almost to their heels. Add to all these natural graces a conical hat, covered with red fringe, an ample tunic with large sleeves, and black satin boots, with a white sole of immense thickness, and it must be evident to all that a European can not compare in appearance with a Chinese."

The Chinese are businessmen by nature, said Huc.

"The Chinese has a passionate love of lucre, he is fond of all kinds of speculation and stock-jobbing, and his mind, full of finesse and cunning, takes delight in combining and calculating the chances of a commercial operation.

"The Chinese, par excellence, is a man installed behind the counter of a shop, waiting for his customers with patience and resignation, and in the intervals of their arrival pondering in his head, and casting up on his little arithmetical machine, the means of increasing his fortune. Whatever may be the nature and importance of his business, he neglects not the smallest profit, the least gain is always welcome, and he accepts it eagerly; greatest of all is his enjoyment, when in the evening, having well closed and barricaded his shop, he can retire into some corner, and there count up religiously the number of his sapecks, and reckon the earnings of the day. The Chinese is born with this taste for traffic, which grows with his growth, and strengthens with his strength.

The first thing a child longs for is a sapeck, the first use that is makes of its speech and intelligence is to learn to articulate the names of coins, when his little fingers are strong enough to hold the pencil, it is with making figures that he amuses himself, and as soon as the tiny creature can speak and walk, he is capable of buying and selling. In China you need never fear sending a child to make a purchase, you may rely on it, he will not allow himself to be cheated. Even the plays to which the little Chinese are addicted are always impregnated with this mercantile spirit, they amuse themselves with keeping shop, and opening little pawnbroking establishments and familiarize themselves thus with the jargon, the tricks, and the frauds of tradesmen."

Upon their arrival at Wuchang, the capital of Hubei Province, the missionaries were virtually ignored by officialdom, and were lodged in small cubicles in a run-down pagoda, a few notches down from the official guest houses to which they had become accustomed.

"The magistrates of the capital took not the slightest notice of us, and, with the exception of some petty officials, no creature came to visit us."

Huc steamed in silence for two days, then decided to confront the mandarins. He put on his ceremonial gown, complete with yellow cap and red girdle, and set off in his palanquin for the Provincial Governor's mansion. He marched into the outer courtyard, and was immediately surrounded by a crowd of attendants "such as usually throng the avenues of the great tribunals, with their sinister hang-dog physiognomies." But he ignored them and marched on. As he passed into a second courtyard, a mandarin stood in Huc's path with his arms out-splayed and asked where he was going.

"We are going to his Excellency the Governor," Huc replied.

"His Excellency the Governor is not there. You can't see the

Governor. Do the Rites permit people to push on in that way to the first magistrate of the province?"

The Mandarin jumped about trying to bar Huc's path, but Huc was determined and pressed on, as the Mandarin retreated in front of him. They reached a set of doors, and the Mandarin threw himself on them in one last desperate attempt to stop the missionaries.

"Woe to you if you do not leave that door open," declared Huc. "If you stop us for a single moment, you are a lost man."

The mandarin shrank away, and Huc made his way without further trouble to the Governor's apartments. He was granted a frosty audience with the Governor, which did, however, result in the party being transferred to more comfortable lodgings in a Buddhist convent on the outskirts of the city.

The next day, Master Ting and the other officials who had accompanied them from Chengdu came to say goodbye. Huc didn't regret parting with Master Ting, but did add:

"At bottom he was not a bad fellow, for a Mandarin, and if one only let him play the Chinese a little, that is to say, finger the sapecks right and left along the road, he was tolerably good-humoured and amiable."

The personal servant they had been given in Chengdu was, however, allowed to continue to accompany them on the rest of their journey to Canton.

The convent prompted Huc to comment on Chinese achievements in the field of art. He thought that the ornamentation and decoration of the convent, as with other Chinese temples, was

"quite in the Chinese taste, and full of caprice and confusion – and the paintings and sculptures have little artistic merit, as the arts of design are very imperfectly cultivated in China. The painters only excel in certain mechanical processes relating to the preparation and

application of colors, in their compositions they pay no attention whatever to perspective, and their landscapes are most distressingly monotonous. Their best performances are in miniatures and water-colors, but though not devoid of a certain kind of beauty, they are still very inferior in style to the most mediocre of European paintings."

Huc was likewise unimpressed by Chinese music.

"Chinese music, it is true, has a certain softness and melancholy in its tones, that pleases you pretty well at first, but it is so intolerably monotonous, that if prolonged it becomes exceedingly irritating to the nerves. The Chinese have no semi-tones in their scale, indeed, one might suppose they merely blew into their instruments, or twanged their strings at random, from the inspiration of the moment, however, it appears they have notes, and though their compositions are doubtless not if much scientific value, you do sometimes hear something like simple melodies in them, such as are heard in the chants of savages and which are more or less agreeable."

With their new escort and refurbished palanquins they started out again, skirting the low-lying lake country, then heading southeast towards the capital of Jiangxi Province, Nanchang, at that time one of the most important trading cities in China due to its position on the main trade route between Canton in the south and central China. As it was "the season of tempests", the officials decided they should travel by road rather than through the region's extensive river and lake system.

The towns they stopped in along this portion of the journey were very poor, the inns were dirty and the food disgusting. At the town of Kuoang-tsi, no food at all was provided, and Huc, in indignation, stormed into the local magistrate's tribunal to demand better treatment. As the two missionaries burst into the main hall of the tribunal, they realized there was a trial in progress, which in China often meant torture.

"All eyes were immediately turned toward us, and a movement of surprise was perceptible throughout the assembly. Two men with great beards, yellow Caps, and red girdles, formed a very surprising apparition. For ourselves, at the first glance we cast into the hall, we felt a cold perspiration come over us, and our limbs tottered under us, we were ready to faint. The first object that presented itself on entering this Chinese judgment hall was the accused – the person on his trial. He was suspended in the middle of the hall, like one of those lanterns, of whimsical form and colossal dimensions often seen in the great pagodas. Ropes attached to a great beam in the roof held him tied by the wrists and feet, so as not to throw the body into the form of a bow. Beneath him stood five or six executioners, armed with rattan rods and leather lashes, in ferocious attitudes, their clothes and faces spotted with blood – the blood of the unfortunate creature, who was uttering stifled groans, while his flesh was torn almost in tatters. The audience present at this frightful spectacle appeared quite at their ease, and our yellow caps excited much more emotion than the spectacle of torture."

The smiling magistrate called for a recess and led them to a small room, where he proceeded to explain the circumstances surrounding the trial. The man being tortured was the leader of a band of ruffians, he said, which had committed more than fifty murders and sundry other crimes using methods of extreme barbarity, including tearing out the tongues and gouging out the eyes of women and children, and cutting people to pieces while still alive.

"These details, frightful as they were, did not surprise us. Our long residence in China had taught us to what degree the instinct of evil is developed among these people."

Maintaining law and order in the Celestial Empire was no easy matter, Huc said, due to the complete lack of religious faith amongst the people, their indifference to morality, and the fact that they have energy only for the amassing of money.

"The immense population of China, depraved by the absence of religious faith and moral education, wholly absorbed in material interests, would not subsist long as a nation, but would be speedily dismembered, were a system of legislation, founded on the principles of absolute justice and right, to be suddenly substituted for the strange one that now governs it. Among a nation of speculators and skeptics, like the Chinese, the social bond is found in the penal, not in the moral law, and the rattan and the bamboo form the sole guarantees for the fulfillment of duty."

Drunkenness and gambling are problems of epidemic proportions, and Chinese are such reckless gamblers that they would even wager their own fingers and cut them off if they lose, said Huc.

"Chinese society has a certain tone of decency and reserve that may very well impose on those who look only at the surface, and judge merely by the momentary impression, but a very short residence among the Chinese is sufficient to show that their virtue is entirely external, their public morality is but a mask worn over the corruption of their manners. We will take care not to lift the unclean veil that hides the putrefaction of this ancient Chinese civilization, the leprosy of vice has spread so completely through this skeptical society, that the varnish of modesty with which it is covered is continually falling off and exposing the hideous wounds which are eating away the vitals of this unbelieving people. Their language is already revoltingly indecent, and the slang of the worst resorts of licentiousness threatens to become the ordinary language of conversation."

Given the amorality of the Chinese people, Huc wondered, should we be surprised by the widespread use of infanticide by parents who want to get rid of baby daughters, and by their many other vices and crimes?

"Should we not, on the contrary, have cause for surprise if it were otherwise? What motive can be capable of arresting the force of passion in men without any religious belief, in whom self-interest is the only rule of good and evil, who live in a skeptical society, under atheistical laws, whose only sanction is the rod and the gallows."

The journey from Wuchang to Nanchang was much less eventful than what had come before, so Huc spent time recounting some of his thoughts on the Chinese and their customs. One day, they were passed on the road by two government couriers, carrying varnished boxes on their backs, containing dispatches for Peking. Huc said China lacked any form of public postal service, but added:

"The Chinese do not suffer much from this state of things, for having scarcely any domestic affections, they do not feel the need of corresponding with their relations and friends. Looking at every thing only on the positive and material side, they have no idea of the tender relations by which two hearts delight to draw near in intimate correspondence, and communicate their joys and their sorrows. They know nothing of the lively emotions that the mere sight of a known handwriting can awaken[.]"

They traveled on in their palanquins and traversed the Yangtze again to the town of Hukou (Mouth of the Lake), situated at the northern tip of the Poyang Lake, where it meets the Yangtze. The Mandarin escorts decided to continue from there to the provincial capital of Nanchang by junk, and a suitable boat was hired.

Huc noted the widespread poverty of Hubei province which they had just left, and commented also on the widespread use of "night soil" as manure:

"When you enter a Chinese hamlet, or approach a farm, you are often struck by a horrible stench that threatens to suffocate you. Not that healthy, though somewhat powerful odor, that escapes from cow-houses and sheep-folds, but an atrocious mixture of all that is disgusting. The Chinese have, indeed, such a passion for human manure of all kinds, and the cuttings of nails, and sell them to farmers to enrich the soil."

They were well received at Nanchang and spent five days there preparing for the last stage of their journey to Canton. They were provided with a Mandarin's river junk and spent 15 delightful days sailing south up the Gan River. Huc spent the time getting his diary up to date in preparation for the task of writing his memoirs. There was little wind, and on the first day, the captain ordered the sailors to make use of the oars to help the junk make headway against the current. The captain came to see the missionaries to inquire whether they had any complaints.

"We are most comfortable," said Huc. "Your delightful vessel is a Paradise, but the motion is very great toward the stern, and the sailors make a great deal of noise in rowing."

"These inconveniences can be removed," said the captain. "I will go and see to it."

A while later, the noise of the oars ceased, but the boat continued to move silently upstream as if carried along by magic. On investigation, Huc found a small boat had been launched and was towing the junk along after it.

They reached the headwaters of the Gan River, and then transferred back to their palanquins for the one-day journey over the mountains dividing Jiangxi Province from Guangdong Province, of which Canton is the capital. Then they boarded another junk at Nanxiong for the faster downstream run to Canton. On the sixth day, they sailed into Canton and saw a sight which moved Huc to tears.

"Among the native vessels of China arose the grand and imposing forms of a steam-ship and several East Indiamen and amidst the flags of all colors that were waving in the air, we perceived those of the United States, of Portugal, and of England. That of France was not among them, but when one has been long at the other side of the world, on an inhospitable soil, in China, in short, it seems that all the people of the West form one great family. The mere sight of a European flag makes the heart beat, for it awakens all the recollections of our country."

It was October 1846 and their trip from Lhasa, high in the Himalayas, had taken six months.

They made contact with an old friend, Mr. Van Bazel, the Dutch consul in Canton, and begged him to send them some newspapers as they had had no news from Europe for more than three years. Van Bazel sent them an enormous bale of papers, along with several bottles of claret.

"We passed the whole night rummaging in this incoherent mass of news that was piled up in the middle of our room, and in one of the very first newspapers that chance threw into our hands, we read an article that we thought rather curious. It was as follows:

'We have lately received intelligence of the lamentable death of the two fathers of the Mongol Tartar Mission.' After a slight glance at the Tartar countries, the author of the article continues:

'A French Lazarist of the name of Huc, took up his abode about three years ago among some Chinese families established in the valley of Black Waters, about six hundred miles from the Great Wall. Another Lazarist, whose name is not known to us, joined him with the purpose of forming a mission for the conversion of the Mongol Buddhists. They studied the Tartar language with the Lamas of the neighboring monasteries, and it appears that, having been regarded as foreign Lamas, they were treated in a friendly manner, especially by the Buddhists, who are very ignorant, and who took the Latin of their breviaries for Sanscrit, which they do not understand, but for which they have much veneration.

'When the Missionaries believed themselves sufficiently instructed in the language they proceeded into the interior, with the intention of commencing the work of conversion. After that period very little was heard of them, until in May last information was received that they had been fastened to the tails of wild horses and dragged to death. The immediate cause of this event is not yet known.' "

Huc was astonished by this news item, and anticipating a more famous comment by Mark Twain several decades later, he added, "We thought we had some reason to doubt its perfect accuracy."

The two missionaries went on from Canton to the Portuguese settlement of Macao at the mouth of the Pearl River, and Huc finally departed the Far East in 1852, returning to Paris, where he died in 1860.

3

LAURENCE OLIPHANT

ELGIN'S MISSION TO CHINA AND JAPAN

LAURENCE OLIPHANT WAS one of the most prolific travel narrative writers of the 19th century, and also a classic Victorian character. He eventually became a mystic and a champion of a Jewish state in Palestine, but his youth was largely spent adventuring in unlikely parts of the world, journeys about which he published a number of books. Born in Cape Town, South Africa in 1829, he followed his father into the legal profession, but at the age of 22, he found his real vocation – a combination of travel and writing. He visited Kathmandu, the capital of the inaccessible Himalayan kingdom of Nepal, and also traveled extensively in Russia. His travelogue of the Crimea, perfectly timed to coincide with the start of the Crimean War, became a bestseller, and soon after he accepted an appointment as personal secretary to Lord Elgin, then Governor-General of Canada, and son of the Elgin who shipped the "Elgin Marbles" from the Parthenon in Athens to the British Museum in London.

He accompanied Elgin on his mission to forcibly open up China and Japan to British trade, and later served time as a Member of Parliament in London. Later still, he came under the spell of T.L. Harris, a religious fanatic in America, to whom Oliphant signed over his entire fortune.

In the 1870s, he led a premature campaign to establish a Jewish state in Palestine, then still under Turkish control. He was not Jewish himself, but declared that the creation of such a state was necessary, "fulfilling prophecy and bringing on the end of the world". Needless to say, the campaign failed and Oliphant moved to the port of Haifa in Palestine, where he wrote a book entitled "Evolutionary Forces Now Active In Man", described as "apparently a plea for purified sex life". He died in 1888.

Compared to the turgid prose of many of his peers, Oliphant's travel writings are very entertaining. His book on the Elgin mission to China and Japan is a lively account of British gunboat diplomacy at its most brazen, and is a good example of the breath-taking arrogance, and contempt for the "natives" which Europeans almost invariably affected in such parts of the world at that time.

The mission started out from London in the Spring of 1857, and became one of the first groups to travel on the new railway linking Alexandria and Cairo across part of the Isthmus of Suez. When they arrived in Ceylon, they received news of the discontent among native Indian troops which would soon explode into the Indian Mutiny. Elgin diverted some of his troops to India to help quell the disturbances, and the Indian troubles delayed the mission for many months.

In Singapore also, the natives were restless. Oliphant refers darkly to recent "occurrences" amongst the Chinese populations of several British possessions in the region including a "treacherous attempt upon the lives of the British residents at Hong Kong", a reference to an attempt by a Chinese baker to kill off the Colony's foreign community by lacing their bread with arsenic.

The Chinese were clearly not to be trusted. But while full of what he saw as their sly, treacherous nature, Oliphant also noted how hard-working the Chinese immigrants in Southeast Asia were compared to the locals. Without Chinese coolies, Malaya, the Philippines, Thailand and Indochina would produce nothing for export at all. In Manila, which the party visited briefly, Oliphant reported that all the best shops were run by Chinese: "The superior industry, intelligence and economical habits of the pure Chinaman give him an immense advantage", he said, over the local Filipinos.

"It is not at all an uncommon thing to see a man coiled up snoring in one corner of his shop, and a mestizo girl stretched luxuriously at full length upon the counter, her beautiful black hair thrown back from her face, falling in wavy massive folds to the ground, and her bosom heaving so softly and regularly with the long-drawn breath of a profound slumber, that, rather than do violence to his aesthetic nature by disturbing sleeping beauty, the purchaser moves gently on to the next shop, and finds a grinning Chinaman...who is imbued with the firm determination, if he does not possess in his shop the article which you do want, to force you to buy from him something you do not."

The Elgin mission had been sent to force China to open itself more fully to foreign trade and contacts. The excuse was an incident the year before involving a Hong Kong- registered ship which had been seized by the Chinese authorities in Hong Kong. "The Arrow incident" as it was called, was a weak pretext at best, as Oliphant almost admits, but the British had decided the situation called for a determined show of strength. Inaction, said Oliphant, would not only impair Britain's prestige, but also be embarrassing. In order to impress the Chinese, the British would occupy Canton, the largest city in southern China, a hundred miles or so up the Pearl River from Hong Kong.

But with most of the mission's troops engaged in India, there was little Elgin could do immediately. For two months during the height of the summer, the party rode at anchor a mile off Hong Kong. Oliphant had nothing but loathing for the small Colony. Even recreational walks around the small town, he said were likely to result in fever.

"The monotony of life is varied by this malady alternating with the boils and dysentery, so that the proverbial hospitality of the merchants at Hong Kong can only be exercised under very adverse influences." Depression and general irritability pervaded the foreign community, he reported, adding: "A large bachelor's party was the extreme limit of gaiety."

Oliphant and his colleagues made the obligatory side trip to Macao, the older Portuguese settlement to the west, as an antidote to the frustrations of upstart Hong Kong.

"Its air of respectable antiquity was refreshing after the somewhat parvenu character with which its ostentatious magnificence invests Hong Kong. In Macao, Oliphant had his first taste of Chinese food, which he enjoyed, "in spite of the novelty of the implements".

They also went for a sail through the islands to the west of Hong Kong and pronounced the scenery to be much like that of the Western Highlands of Scotland. Their ship then turned north into the Pearl River estuary.

"It was our first introduction to Chinese scenery: numerous villages dotted the river banks, some of them utterly destroyed and depopulated either by rebels or ourselves."

The most conspicuous structure in these villages was a high square tower. Oliphant said it was significant of the character of the Chinese race that these were not the strongholds of a local feudal baron, "but of some old usurer who needs a fortress for the preservation of sundry goods and chattels which he holds in pawn for the credit of his victims. The number of these pawnbroking towers inspires one with rather a low estimate of the solvency of the community."

Finally, early in December 1857, an awaited contingent of marines arrived, making an attack on Canton feasible at last. Just for the record, the British sent the Chinese High Commissioner in Canton, Yeh Ming-shen, an ultimatum which deplored the "attitude of hostility and dislike which the people and authorities of Canton have maintained in their dealings with foreigners", and demanded compensation for losses sustained by British subjects. Yeh rejected the ultimatum, and the British force moved up the Pearl River towards Canton, flotillas of Chinese boat-dwellers fleeing before them.

The British anchored off Whampoa, a town a few miles downriver from Canton. The local villagers generally seemed unconcerned by the arrival of the foreigners or by the threat they posed to Canton, but the British party decided "it was desirable to take our evening walks armed with revolvers," Oliphant said.

The British had warned the Chinese Commissioner Yeh that they would begin shelling Canton on Boxing Day, December 26, if he did not agree to the demands in the ultimatum, but they held off until December 28. "It will thus be seen that every opportunity was afforded to the authorities to yield, and to the people to provide for their own safety and the security of their property," Oliphant commented.

The bombardment began shortly after day-break and continued for twenty-seven hours. British and French troops landed that day, and Oliphant noted: "As I observe in the French papers that our gallant allies have claimed some credit for being the first to land on the 28th, it is only fair to state the amount of risk they incurred in landing at a spot which had been in our possession since the previous day."

The troops advanced into hilly rice paddy country. "It was just the country for skirmishing in, and had our enemy not been contemptible, they might have harassed us seriously as we advanced. As it happens, what little danger there was arose rather from a species of treachery than from open warfare."

The surrounding hills were crowded with spectators as the British and French approached Yeh's fort, "the capture of which it had been arranged should complete the first day's operations." The next day, the foreigners continued on to Canton, meeting little resistance from Chinese troops. They took control of the city, and took Commissioner Yeh prisoner. (Yeh was shipped off to Calcutta as a prisoner of war and died in India.)

Taking Canton was one thing, ruling it was entirely another, not least, Oliphant said, because its population contained "a larger proportion of trained thieves and vagabonds than any in the world".

The foreigners had a force of about 5,000 soldiers at their disposal to administer this strange Oriental city, and only two men who could speak Chinese. They quickly gave up the idea of trying to run Canton, and decided there was no alternative but to let the Chinese continue to run it themselves. Looters, both Chinese and foreign, were having a grand time, but Oliphant said the English sailors did not have the best eye for value.

"Our simple tars presented a marked contrast in their looting propensities to their more prudent comrades among the allies. These latter possessed a wonderful instinct for securing portable articles of value, and, while honest Jack was flourishing down the street with a broad grin of triumph on his face, a bowl of gold-fish under one arm, and a cage of canary-birds under the other, honest Jean, with a demure countenance, and no external display, was conveying his well-lined pockets to the waterside."

The population of Canton gradually got used to the idea of foreign occupation. People returned to their houses, and shops re-opened. Oliphant described the transformation of one of

Canton's larger thoroughfares:

"As the 'Avenue of Benevolence and Love' was more frequented, it became a less agreeable lounge, and the already narrow streets were still farther diminished in breadth by large tubs full of live fish, baskets of greens, sea chestnuts, yams, and bamboo root. Cooking-stoves were erected, and elaborately cooked viands hissed and sputtered on the heated iron, titillating with their savory odor the nostril of the hungry passenger. Open coppers steamed and bubbled, and delicate morsels danced on the surface, round tables were daintily set out with pastry of divers patterns, and presided over by croupiers, who jerked reeds in a box, or spun a ball something after the fashion of roulette, thus enabling the dinner-seeker to combine the exhilarating excitement of the gambler with the Epicurean enjoyment of the gourmand, the consideration that they had cost him nothing adding additional zest to his gastronomic pleasures. It might so happen, on the other hand, that one unkind turn of the wheel of fortune sent him supperless to bed."

But Oliphant was far from attracted by this scene.

"After the first novelty has worn off, there is nothing to make a promenade in the streets of a Chinese town attractive. The foulest odors assail the olfactories. The most disgusting sights meet the eye – objects of disease, more loathsome than anything to be seen in any other part of the world, jostle against you. Coolies staggering under coffins, or something worse, recklessly dash their loads against your shins, you suspect every man that touches you of a contagious disease, and the streets themselves are wet, slippery, narrow, tortuous and crowded."

Oliphant was also disgusted in the extreme by the sight of Chinese women.

"When to their natural ugliness is added the deformity of feet and apparent entire absence of arms – for a Chinese woman seldom makes use of the sleeves of her jacket, any thing more unprepossessing than the lady part of the community could not be well conceived."

Once in control of Canton, the British and French representatives, along with those of the United States and Russia, sent a note to Peking demanding that an Imperial representative be sent to Shanghai to negotiate with them. No satisfactory reply was forthcoming, so Lord Elgin decided in February that the only way to solve the problem was to exercise "a moral pressure of a military description" in the neighborhood of the Imperial capital.

The envoys and their party left Canton, and sailed northeast along the China coast, first to Amoy, and then to Shanghai. The highest-ranking Chinese official in the city was absent, and so the foreigners decided to force themselves on the most senior Chinese representative in the immediate vicinity, the Governor of Kiangsu Province, who resided in the nearby city of Soochow (Suzhou).

The party was uncertain about whether they would be able to get to Soochow, fifty miles to the west of Shanghai. The city had never been officially visited by Europeans, and had only been seen, Oliphant said, by a few Europeans disguised as Chinese or concealed in boats. On February 24, the party, consisting of seventeen boats, set off for Soochow through the maze of rivers and canals which criss-crossed the low-lying region of east China.

Probably the most important member of the party, the only one who could speak Chinese, was Mr. Horatio Nelson Lay, 25 years of age and already the Inspector of Imperial Customs at Shanghai. In 1861, he was to become the founder and first Inspector-General of the Chinese customs service, which regulated trade through the fourteen ports then open to foreign trade, collecting tariff charges for the Chinese government until well into the 20th century.

The trip took them through the Grand Canal, the world's longest man-made waterway, constructed hundreds of years before to transport grain from southern China to the Imperial capital in the north. At the time Oliphant saw it, some stretches of the canal had not been used for several years, due to floods and to the Taiping Rebellion, which raged back and forth around Soochow during the 1850s and early 1860s. The banks of the canal were lined, he said, with enormous imperial grain-junks, which were rotting away.

"They look like so many stranded arks going to decay: this is their inevitable destiny, as the profane vulgar are not allowed to touch Imperial property."

Oliphant's comparison of the bustling sections of the Grand Canal with London traffic is delightful:

"There were as many different varieties of boats here as there are of vehicles in Fleet Street, and the water-way was as inconveniently crowded as that celebrated thoroughfare usually is. Ferry-boats plied as briskly and were as heavily loaded as omnibuses, heavy cargo- boats lumbered along and got in every body's way, just as brewers' drays do. Light tanka-boats, with one or two passengers, and deftly worked by a single oar astern, cut in and out like hansoms. And there were large passage-boats with accommodation for travellers on long journeys, that plied regularly between Soo-chow, Hang-chow, Chang-chow, and other distant cities and that created the same sort of sensation as they passed as did the Brighton Age or Portsmouth Telegraph in days gone by. Gentlemen's private carriages were here represented by gorgeous mandarin junks, with the huge umbrella on the top, and a gong at the entrance to the cabin, beaten at intervals by calfless flunkies. Other junks there were, more gaudily painted even than these, from whence issued shrill voices, and sounds of noisy laughter and music. There was the costermonger in his humble substitute for a donkey-cart, a small covered canoe, which looked like a coffin and in which he sat alone, forcing it speedily through the water with a pair of oars, one of which he worked astern with his hand, and the other at the side with his feet. The race of scavengers lived in flat punts, and, scooping up the mud and rubbish from the bottom of the canal, discharged it into them, where it was immediately examined by a number of ducks kept on board for the purpose, who picked out all that was worth eating, and what they rejected was then inspected by their owners for waifs and strays that had been lost from junks, and then taken to fatten the land. But the most curious appearance was presented by the boats which carried the fishing cormorants, solemnly perched in successive rows on stages projecting from the sides, they looked like a number of gentlemen in black on the platform at a meeting of a grave and serious character."

They arrived outside the Soochow city walls, which formed a perfect square surrounded on all sides by canals. A messenger appeared on the bank with a note from the Provincial Governor Chaou, asking them to wait outside the city walls where he would come to meet them.

"But, anxious to get inside the city walls, we pressed on, threading our way in line along the densely thronged canal, and attracting to its banks and the roofs of the houses crowds of eager spectators, not accustomed to see British, French, and American flags flaunting impudently under their very windows. We appeared so suddenly before the water-gate called 'Foomun' that the officials, had they wished it, would scarcely have had time to shut it. However, they contented themselves with making the most frantic gesticulations and expressive signs to us to turn back, but we put on an air of the most obtuse stolidity, and pushed vehemently on, my boat, which happened to be leading, carrying away in the hurry some of the grille which formed part of the gate.

"Once in the city, we did not venture on an exploration of the lanes of water, which like those of Venice, opened up in divers directions, but moored at once in a retired spot under the walls. We were not long, however, left in quiet. Almost immediately a dense crowd collected on both sides of the canal, deeply interested in the proceedings of the barbarians. Whenever any of us moved from one boat to another, a general titter of astonishment and curiosity was heard, but they manifested no semblance of dislike or hostility toward us, and were infinitely more respectable in their behavior than an English mob would have been under similar circumstances."

A detail of Chinese soldiers approached and escorted them to the residence of the Governor, who greeted them politely at the door of his audience room. The senior British representative, a Mr. Meadows, informed the Governor that they were carrying messages for the Chinese Prime Minister from the four allies, which he hoped he would convey to Peking immediately.

"The covering dispatch to himself he opened and read, a crowd of attendants collecting round him and making themselves acquainted with its contents over his shoulder. As we desired that the whole proceeding should be invested with as much publicity as possible, this mode of conducting business, though rather unusual in Western diplomacy, was quite in accordance with our wishes."

Oliphant described Governor Chaou as "the best specimen of a Chinese gentleman I had yet seen in China," but did not lose an opportunity to comment on what he perceived as wily inscrutability:

"A Chinaman has a wonderful command of feature, he

generally looks most pleased when he has least reason to be so, and maintains an expression of imperturbable politeness and amiability when he is secretly regretting devoutly that he can not bastinado you to death." (Bastinado is an Spanish word meaning to torture someone by caning them on the soles of their feet.)

The audience over, the party returned to Shanghai. Oliphant took another side-trip to the city port of Ningpo, where he attended a Chinese opera performance in a local temple. As expected, he was not impressed.

"The disagreeable necessity of being obliged to form one of a dense crowd of very odoriferous Chinamen prevented my staying very long, nor was the plot of so refined a nature as to render the performance attractive, but the acting was in some instances clever."

On a visit to another temple in the area, the priests treated him to tea and fingered his strange European garments in wonder.

"I have generally found gloves and corduroy trousers to be the most striking objects of dress to the uncivilized mind, shooting-boots are also curiosities. Our entertainers, however, were becoming accustomed to Europeans, and had evidently smoked a few cigars in their lives before, but they were particularly amused by my Madras servant, apparently a specimen of humanity heretofore unknown to them, they took him to look at the hideous black deities which guarded the entrance of the temple, a compliment to his personal appearance at which they chuckled hugely, but which he did not seem to appreciate."

On April 10, a suitably impressive fleet of gun-boats having been assembled, the foreign representatives left Shanghai heading north. They crossed the Yellow Sea, rounded the Shangdong peninsula, and sailed into the Beihai Gulf, then known as the Gulf of Pechelee. The intention was to sail up the Hai River towards Peking to cow the Chinese into accepting treaty terms dictated by the foreign powers. But the naval force was deemed too small to force its way up the river, and so it was decided to wait for more reinforcements. As the foreigners rode at anchor in the shallow brown waters of the Gulf for a month, the Chinese worked to strengthen the forts guarding the mouth of the river. More ships arrived, and on May 20, the foreigners attacked the forts and took them easily. The way to Peking was now open, and they became the first foreign ships to sail up the Hai River to Tientsin, a large trading port to the east of Peking.

"Towards evening the mud villages became more numerous: their entire populations turned out as the leading gun-boats passed, and saluted them with profound and reverential obeisances, then squatted in a long blue line upon the river's bank, and gazed in awestruck wonderment as our ardent little craft, defying wind and tide, puffed steadily along, a slight commotion under her stern being the only external evidence to the Celestial eye of the demon that was propelling her."

It was a classic example of gunboat diplomacy, and the natives were suitably impressed. The villagers, Oliphant said, were clearly under the impression that the foreigners were on their way to Peking to overthrow the Manchus and establish a new dynasty. The Imperial Court sent word that an Imperial representative would be sent to Tientsin for negotiations, and the party landed in the suburbs of Tientsin where the local officials made available the Temple of Supreme Felicity on the river bank as living quarters for the foreigners during their stay.

"The personnel of the two missions were accommodated in the temple, and other buildings all inclosed within one outer wall. A partition wall, however, divided us from our allies. They occupied a number of detached summer-houses, dotted about a garden. We established ourselves in the innermost recesses of the temple, our bedrooms furnished with sacred pigs and bronzes, in which smouldered eternal fire (until we came and allowed it to go out), our slumbers presided over by grinning deities with enormous stomachs, or many-armed goddesses, with heads encircled in a blaze of golden or rather brass flame. The perfume of incense still clung to these sacred purlieus. Would it had been the only odor to which our nostrils were subjected! Now began the process commonly known as "shaking down" into our quarters: altars were turned into wash-hand-stands, looking-glasses were supported against little gods, tables, chairs, and beds were indented for upon certain venerable citizens, who had been appointed by the authorities to attend to our wants. Doubtless they must have wondered much at many of our demands, and some of them – as, for instance, tubs – they never succeeded in satisfying."

The American and Russian envoys, tagging along after the Anglo-French force, had more difficulty finding accommodation. They chose a suitable house on the river bank, but "the proprietor made a novel proposition in the shape of an offer of 6,000 dollars if they would not rent it." The offer was declined, and the foreigners occupied the house anyway, paying the owner "a handsome rent" for its use.

Their stay near Tientsin lasted about a month and Oliphant and his colleagues decided they needed horses in order to extend the range of their explorations during their stay.

"We therefore sent in a requisition for a certain number of steeds, and, after some delay, were furnished with what appeared the scum of the stables of Tientsin. These were indignantly rejected, and we ultimately obtained six very respectable ponies, and six very uncomfortable Chinese saddles, very hard and angular, and garnished with extensive drapery, and an awkward bolster-shaped protuberance in front. To these uncouth contrivances, however, we ultimately became accustomed, and I had minutely explored the country round Tientsin within a radius of about six miles before we left it."

A meeting between the Imperial commissioner, Kweiliang, and the foreign envoys was arranged at The Temple of Oceanic Influences about two miles outside Tientsin. The foreign entourage, consisting of twelve sedan chairs, a guard of honor of 150 marines and the band of the British man-of-war Calcutta, made its way there in procession through the narrow streets, watched by a spellbound Chinese crowd. The envoys were met by the Chinese commissioners in the courtyard of the mansion, and led into a meeting room where they were seated at a table. Lord Elgin announced that he had come with full powers of negotiation from his Sovereign, and asked whether Kweiliang had done the same. This was always a sticking point in Chinese-Western relations. The Chinese produced an Imperial decree conferring large powers on Kweiliang, but Elgin found the commissioner had not been provided with a seal of office. A show of displeasure was called for, so Elgin immediately stood up and left, with the Chinese commissioners chasing after him.

"Lord Elgin had arrived in Tientsin as the representative of a nation whose dignity had been outraged", said Oliphant. "It had been necessary to have recourse to violence, and to force an entry into the country, to obtain satisfaction for insults: and any symptom of reluctance to grant a stern, uncompromising bearing doubly necessary."

The Chinese, thoroughly alarmed, asked for Mr. Lay, the Shanghai Inspector of Customs and linguist, to help reach a compromise and eventually the commissioners were provided with powers acceptable to the foreigners. Negotiations proceeded. A diplomatic triumph now seemed assured, but Oliphant was sorry the Chinese acquiesced to the foreign demands so readily – a more unyielding attitude from the Chinese would have given the foreigners an excuse to force their way into Peking, still a closed city.

Oliphant praised the locals of Tientsin for their respectful behavior towards the foreigners, until one day a crowd pelted and hooted at the British Admiral while he was out walking. The next day, a certain Captain Dew and a colleague were "attacked by the mob, who, however, entertained too great a respect for barbarian prowess to press them very close, and they escaped with only the loss of a favorite dog of Captain Dew's, and the hat of that gallant officer."

Incensed at this insolence, Captain Dew led a party of British marines back to where the outrage had occurred. His hat was handed back to him, but the British decided that, in view of the impropriety of the behavior of people in that part of the city, it would be necessary to take a number of householders prisoner. A few shopkeepers were seized, marched off by the marines, and kept in confinement for one night, during which Captain Dew's dog, a retriever, swam to the ship on which his master was staying.

Oliphant found Tientsin slightly less obnoxious than the cities of southern China he had visited. The streets were wider, and "the visitor could pursue his exploratory investigations without having his nostrils assailed at every turn by the indescribably foul odors of the south". Even so, he describes the city as "the most squalid, impoverished-looking place we had ever been in".

In the markets, he found some Manchester-made cloth, but was pessimistic about the opportunities for further trade.

"In contemplating the population of Tientsin with a practically commercial eye, the problem is not whether they want clothes, but whether they have money enough to buy them ... In no part of the world have I ever witnessed a more squalid, diseased population than that which seemed rather to infest than inhabit the suburbs of the city. Filth, nakedness, and itch were the prevailing characteristics. The banks of the river swarmed with men who lived entirely on the garbage and offal that were flung from the ships, or were swept up by the tide from the city. There was an eddy just in front of our yamun in which dead cats, etc., used to gyrate, and into which stark naked figures were constantly plunging in search of some delicate morsel. Their clothing generally consisted of a piece of mat or tattered sacking, which they wore, not round their waist, but thrown negligently over their shoulders – it was difficult to divine for what purpose, as decency was ignored, and in the month of June warmth was not a desideratum. Cutaneous diseases of the most loathsome character met the eye in the course of the shortest walk, and objects so frightful that their vitality seemed a mockery of existence shocked the coarsest sensibilities.

"Upon several occasions I saw life ebbing from some wretched suffer as he lay at his post of mendicancy. One old woman, in particular, attracted my attention. She used to lie motionless on a mat in the centre of the road, a diseased skeleton. She had just strength enough to clutch at cash that was flung at her. One day this strength seemed to have failed: I looked closer, and she was dead. A few hours after, I repassed, but her place knew her no more: she had been carried away and cast upon a dung-heap." Oliphant summed up his feelings about the city by adding:

"As if in ironical allusion to the misery which the living seemed to endure, almost the only pretty spots near Tientsin were the burial-places." As to the young women, a constant source of interest to Oliphant, some of the girls of Tienstin he thought pretty, "but as a general rule, the women generally seen were hideous".

On his rambles through the countryside around Tientsin, Oliphant was pleased to find well-tended kitchen-gardens, vineyards, and plenty of green vegetation. But towards the end of June, luckily after the harvest, a locust plague descended on the area.

"Locust- hunting was a favorite and profitable occupation among the juvenile part of the community. I had the curiosity to eat one, and thought it not unlike a periwinkle."

On June 26, 1858, as the locusts swarmed around the city, Lord Elgin and his Chinese counterparts signed the Treaty of Tientsin which, among other things, gave foreign envoys the right to reside in Peking for the first time, and established the right of foreigners, including Christian missionaries, to travel through the interior of China.

The Forces of Right having finally triumphed over Chinese obstinacy, Lord Elgin, with Oliphant in tow, sailed off to negotiate a similar treaty with the Japanese Empire.

4

JOHN "CHINA" THOMSON

ILLUSTRATIONS OF CHINA AND ITS PEOPLE

BORN THE SON OF a Scottish tobacco spinner, John Thomson (1837-1921) took a crucial detour away from a modest career in the family business when, in the early 1850s, he accepted an apprenticeship at a local optical and scientific instrument maker. After supplementing his professional training with night courses in subjects like chemistry and math, he was soon a good photographer – so proficient that by 1861 he had already been invited to join the Royal Scottish Society of Arts. Then, feeling the tug of Empire, which at the time was luring away many young Scotsmen, he abandoned his cushy society circle to head to Singapore, where his brother William had already set up shop.

Together with William, he ran an optical instruments business for several years, supplementing his income by taking portraits of European traders in Singapore. The photography eventually took center stage, and Thomson opened his own studio. Around the same time, alongside his professional pursuits, he became interested in using photography to document the street life and landscape of Singapore. He also began to travel widely around Asia on photographic expeditions, going to Siam (Thailand) – where he photographed the royal family – and the Cambodian temples at Angkor Wat – where, after nearly dying from jungle fever, he became the first person to ever photograph them.

In 1867, he shifted his base to Hong Kong and began a five-year period of travel and photography in China. He covered wide swathes of the country, going as far north as Manchuria, as far west as Szechuan (Sichuan) and as far east as Formosa (Taiwan). His subjects ranged from portraits of the elite merchants to those of poor laborers, as well as architecture and landscapes.

These photography expeditions were dangerous and exhausting; besides the fact that the travel itself was often risky and uncomfortable, Thomson also needed to cart along delicate, cumbersome cameras and equipment, a makeshift darkroom and volatile chemicals. Adding to his difficulties, his human subjects were often deeply suspicious of Westerners, especially Westerners with cameras. They were often extremely resistant to having their photos taken, believing the whirring lens to be a new type of weapon or a means of robbing them of their souls. Never seeming to catch a break, even when only innocently snapping landscapes, Thomson often found himself in sticky situations, sometimes even being chased by angry mobs convinced that he was sabotaging their land with his mysterious machinery.

Nonetheless, he was not put off by these many challenges, and his extensive work documenting China delighted the Victorian arm-chair travelers of the time, and remains a valuable contribution to the fields of photography and sinology. Returning to the UK permanently after his travels in China, he quickly established himself as an expert in the use of photography in fieldwork, becoming a prominent member and frequent lecturer at organizations such as the Royal Geographic Society and the Royal Ethnological Society. He continued with his photographic work in the UK as well. From 1876 to 1877, he collaborated with radical journalist Adolphe Smith on the monthly magazine Street Life London, which documented in text and image the lives of

London's street people. In fact, it is for this project, rather than his extensive Asian work, that Thomson is best remembered, and he is now seen as a pioneer of social documentary photography. His other projects were less noteworthy: he returned to the lucrative portraiture work with which he had begun his career, and – after moving his studio to the swish surroundings of London's Mayfair – established himself as a photographer to high-society. Eventually leaving the studio in the hands of his children, he retired quietly to his native Edinburgh, where he died in 1921.

Thomson's photographic work in China is significant not only as a visual record of the late Qing Dynasty era, but also as an example of his pioneering methods of anthropological photography. As some of the first photos to document all strata of society, and a variety of urban and rural scenes, they paint a rich portrait of the country. Never shying away from recording scenes of poverty or dilapidation, he avoided the narrow "picturesque" views so popular with his contemporaries. He also employed novel techniques, which revolutionized the field of photography and enhanced his narrative on China: for instance, his street-scene and landscape photos often contained human figures (up to then, due to the costs of materials, most photographers only allowed paying customers to appear in their photos), and he focused on activities (such as trades-people at work), in order to give a more nuanced view of Chinese society.

While these photographic contributions have often been studied, Thomson's written work is often largely passed over. This is unfortunate, as his engaging style and vivid descriptions, both of the places he explored and of the challenges he encountered as a photographer, make his narratives equally rich sources on 19th century China.

In his book Through China with a Camera, his interest in and knowledge of Chinese society and politics, as well as his unique understanding of the country's artistic potential, allow him to be an engaging narrator. His photographer's instincts often lead him to "zoom in" on details that other writers of the time skimmed over. While his position is often that of a typical gentleman of the Enlightenment – promoting Western science, technology and governance in China and a rejection of its "backward looking" Confucian traditions – his obvious concerns for the poor and the suffering he observes indicate an empathy that was seldom found in the work of his more "rational" contemporaries.

From the outset, Thomson made it clear that his trusty companion, the camera, was not to be dismissed as a silly new-fangled gadget. Citing the disbelief with which Marco Polo's travel tales were met, he built a case for the camera as an insurance policy, guaranteeing the veracity of the fabulous stories he was about to report. To support this position, he began by elaborating a view of China's incredibly long history and its traditions – Confucianism, Buddhism and the complex educational and governmental system based around Imperial examinations – which were so "foreign" to his Western readers. While he unrepentantly argued that all of these ancient systems were utterly corrupt and incompetent, and needed to be "updated" by Western "modernity", he also emphasized that, despite increasing Western influence in the country, the people still, in many ways, persisted as they always had:

"A native scholar once remarked that it takes more than a thousand years to introduce a new tone into the Chinese language. Should this estimate afford some clue to the ratio of political and social progress, it is difficult to limit the time required to cast off the chrysalis of antiquity in which the Empire is shrouded."

In short, the traditions and habits of ancient China still endured despite Western intervention and influence, and his mission was to document it with both pen and camera.

His travels began in Hong Kong, his home and commercial base at the time, and a place in his view that had been somewhat rescued from the "ravages" of ancient Chinese customs, and was in turn itself now rescuing the rest of China.

"This spot, moored to our little island by an electric cable that sweeps half round the globe, rises like a political beacon out of the China Sea, and has by no means been without its influence in preventing the Tartar dynasty from foundering, in maintaining peace and casting the light of a higher civilization over some dark corners of the Flowery Land."

But he candidly lamented the city's diseased slums and the precarious existence of its boat people, living on frail, leaky crafts bobbing in the harbor. He put these down to the fact that "the natives, the best of whom still cling to their old superstitions, are in the mid-stage of evolution."

He believed such ills would disappear as soon as they were sufficiently educated and supported this view by appraising the development of the city's increasingly sophisticated photography and portraiture scene. Though neither was fully "evolved", he was impressed by their progress.

On photography, he found the practitioners to be technically skilled, but disapproved of their aesthetic choices.

"Some of the specimens of photographic art displayed in doorways are fairly good, while others are the most hideous caricatures of the human face that it is possible for the camera to produce."

It was mainly the framing of such portraits he disliked, not the actual photographic work, and this he attributed principally to the Chinese desire for symmetry and a dislike of shadow. Though not yet "developed", there was potential once the "native superstitions" about poses had been cast aside. On portraiture, he was more reserved. He grudgingly admired the speedy assembly-line methods of the hack painters who marketed their wares to European travellers, but dismissed their work as shoddy. He detected signs of talent in their work but thought it was wasted on second-rate pieces.

Leaving Hong Kong and its busy progress towards modernity, Thomson made his first excursion into "China proper", taking a short boat trip up the Pearl River into Guangdong Province. His first stop was Fatshan, today rendered in English as Foshan, which he calls the "Sheffield of Cathay" due to its booming cutlery and hardware industry.

Thomson was at first baffled by the success of the low-quality goods produced in the factories: "It appeared strange to me after examining the native wares, that similar articles of superior English make had done so little to supplant the industry of the Fatshan factories," but after reflection, he concluded that exceedingly cheap prices and better understanding of the local market gave them an edge. He also admitted that Fatshan had its charms, especially the floating, flower-covered teahouses.

As his boat moved beyond Fatshan and continued upriver, the countryside reminded Thomson pleasantly of the rolling hills of the Scottish lowlands, and he decided to take his first photograph on the mainland. But the shot was not to be, as gun-shy locals, who had recently seen more than their fair share of foreign combat troops, intervened.

"I prepared to take a photograph, and my intention was to include a group of old women who were gossiping and drawing water; but when they saw my instrument pointed towards their hamlet, they fled in alarm, and spread abroad the report that the foreigners had returned and were preparing to bombard the settlement."

It took much smoothing-over with the local chief before

Thomson and his travel companions could go in peace. Other adventures during that trip to included a near-death experience in quicksand, a monastery full of opium-pushing monks, a visit to a lavish foreign settlement built on a sinking pile of mud and an encounter with local farmers attempting to accrue free manure by building deluxe outhouses for travelers along their property.

Thomson decided to head back for a night's rest in the city of Canton. While pausing to take a photo on a riverbank, he was mobbed by local thugs, unceremoniously tossed into the river and later rescued by two ladies in a canoe.

Safe in Canton, Thomson began his descriptions of the city by rubbishing previous reports:

"Canton is by no means the densely packed London in China which some have made it out to be", noting its puniness and "straggling" suburbs. He conceded that "Notwithstanding the narrowness of the streets of Canton, they are extremely picturesque; more especially those in which we find the old curiosity-shops, the silversmiths and the silk-mercers, where the signboards present a most attractive display of brilliant and varied colors."

The artisan quarter held the greatest pull for him and he was impressed by the quality of workmanship he observed in a number of trades such as embroidery and metallurgy, but was saddened by the lack of education, poor working conditions and low wages. Many artisans worked for only a few pennies a day, sleeping in their workshops at night, and – despite their obvious artistic talents – never receiving any training beyond the skills their work directly required.

Thomson presciently proposed:

"It will be seen from the foregoing notes that skilled labor is so cheap in China as to give artisans a great advantage in all those various branches of native industry which find a market abroad;

and this will one day render the clever, careful and patient Chinaman a formidable rival to European manufacturers." Testing his own hand at the kind of work, Thomson tried to snap a shot of a Cantonese garden that he believed matched the idyllic scenes they embossed on their pottery and fabrics. The garden was the "China pictured to us in our schoolboy days. Here we see model Chinese gardening; drooping willows, shady walks and sunny lotus-pools, on which gilded barges float. Here, too, spanning a lake, stands the well-known willow-pattern bridge, with a pavilion hard by...I photographed this willow-pattern bridge, but when I look at my picture, I find it falls far short of the scene on our soup-plates."

Pushing on to nearby Macao, then a Portuguese colony, Thomson was surprised to find it looking so much like a European seaside resort nestled so close to the intensely Chinese towns beyond in Kwang-Tung.

"In that pretty watering-place we may enjoy the cool sea-breezes, and almost fancy, when promenading the broad Praya Grande, as it sweeps round a bay truly picturesque, that we have been suddenly transported to some ancient continental town."

But for all its quaint European scenery, it was a city beset by problems. Trade was languishing and gambling houses were overabundant. More closely inspecting the cityscape, Thomson detected, with his photographer's eye, cracks in the picturesque veneer:

"The main streets in Macao are deserted. The houses there are painted in a variety of strange colors, some of the windows being fringed with a rim of red, which gives them the look of inflamed eyes in the painted cheeks of the dwellings."

He went on to critique the overblown lifestyles of Macanese society and the garish second-rate art on sale. It was, he felt, a city of pleasant first impressions and rather distasteful, charmless substance.

Heading back into the mainland, he found it equally unappealing. Rousing himself quite early one morning, he headed out in hopes of photographing a particularly beautiful bridge, which was designed in what he termed "break neck architecture" because of the many dwellings cobbled precariously on to its spans. Anti-foreign sentiment was abroad in the town – foreigners were often attacked with sticks and stones, and the British had abandoned their consulate there due to local violence, so Thomson intended to arrive before the morning markets started, but he was too late:

"I had just time to show myself and take a photograph, when a howling multitude came rushing down to where I stood near my boat on the shore. Amid a shower of missiles I unscrewed my camera, with the still undeveloped photograph inside, took the apparatus under my arm, and presenting my iron-pointed tripod to the rapidly approaching foe, backed into the river and scrambled on board the boat."

Deciding to leave such photo-hostile territory, Thomson headed eastwards up the coast to the city of Amoy, today called Xiamen. His first image of the city from the harbor was inviting:

"At Amoy, the houses in the native quarter are huddled together like a crowd of sightseers, all eager to stand in the front row along the water's edge."

On landing, the sights became less appealing.

"Every second shop reeks with a smell of roasting fat and onions. Mangy dogs and lean pigs yelp and grunt as we disturb their occupations: these are the sanitary authorities of the locality and to them the duty falls to clear up the refuse and garbage."

Intense poverty, a rampant infanticide problem, an acute shortage of graves, high taxes and brutal political tactics all further soured Thomson's opinion. Yet, he ended his stay in the city on a positive note, his spirits again cheered by the efforts of local artisans, in whom he saw hope for China's redemption:

"My sketch of Amoy has thus far been a dark one, and yet the true picture is not without some glances of light striking down even into the lowest quarters of the town. Thus, in one of my many perambulations I came to a very narrow and very dark lane, where I found the humble tenants of the houses engaged in what, to me, was quite a new industry. Men, women and children were all busily occupied in the manufacture of most beautiful artificial flowers. I entered shop after shop, and everywhere found thousands of flowers spread out on trays, and each one so lifelike that it might almost be mistaken for nature herself. I bought a great many of these flowers from a man in a very mean shop indeed. He was extremely poor, and he asked me for an advance of money, offering to furnish security if I wished. I lent him a few dollars without troubling him for securities; and though I knew nothing about him, he carried out the transaction with the most scrupulous honesty."

A few days later, Thomson left Amoy on a steamer bound for Formosa (Taiwan) with his friend Dr. Maxwell, a medical missionary. Despite being incredibly seasick, Thomson managed to elicit lurid tales of the island's native cannibal tribes from the crew. Upon landing in Formosa he made straight for the office of the island's "Taotai" (governor) to request permission to photograph in the interior. Armed with an official invitation, he arrived at the office full of confidence, but was coldly requested to wait outside the palace while the officials considered his request. Thomson patiently waited while a curious crowd collected to inspect him.

"I found myself surrounded by the idle crowd that is always certain to collect about a stranger in China — whence the gazers came, and whither they would go, would be difficult to tell —

and all sorts of conjectures being thrown out as to the nature of my business. A little naked boy, with a face full of perfectly untutored innocent curiosity, ventured a trifle too near, so I leaned slightly forward and frowned at him. Bursting into a fit of screaming terror he fled from the yamen, while the mob looked grave, and wondered what devilry I could have practiced on the child."

With excellent timing, official attendants, "who wore the usual conical hats with red feathers that suggested the idea of flames burning through the top of an extinguisher", arrived to escort him into the palace. Once inside, he was surprised to be greeted in fluent English by a former business acquaintance from Hong Kong, who also happened to be the nephew of the Taotai. Feigning chumminess, the old "pal" did his best to get Thomson to divulge the "secret mission" of his visit to the palace. Thomson repeated innocently (and truthfully) that his only business was to request permission to travel into the interior and photograph the native tribes. The nephew didn't buy the story, and the Taotai was equally suspicious, both of them believing that no one would risk the danger. But after warning Thomson of the cruel, bloodthirsty indigenous tribes, he was grudgingly granted him permission in exchange for portraits.

Permission thus acquired, Thomson and Maxwell, who hoped to open new missions in the interior, and a band of coolies lugging his photographic equipment headed inland. The terrain was craggy and treacherous, the roads terrible and the Chinese settlements smelly and dilapidated, but nevertheless, Thomson seemed to enjoy the adventure. After much climbing, they began to pass through Pepohoan villages. Originally peaceful plain-dwellers, the Pepohoans had been pushed far into the mountains by the invading Chinese over the past two centuries, and though still not as violent as the cannibalistic tribes further inland, they had begun to defend their position vigorously to avoid further encroachment. However, their experiences with the Dutch, who had colonized the island in the 16th century, had given the Pepohoans a positive opinion of Europeans, and they warmly welcomed Thomson and co. Throughout the day, the party was greeted with gentle calls of "peace be with you" as they hiked past the Pepohoan settlements. The further they moved inland, the more astounding the scenery became as well. Striking contrasts of lush jungle, stark cliffs and waterfalls made for particularly photogenic landscapes. As Thomson described it, "I could now understand what the Portuguese meant when they named the island Formosa [which means 'beautiful']; and yet what we saw here was but the foreshadowing of the wilder grandeur of the mountain scenery inland."

After practically dragging Thomson away from his camera, the group arrived at their lodgings for the night in a Pepohoan village. Thomson bonded with the locals over their mutual appreciation of tobacco:

"Here the men, women and children were all provided with bamboo tobacco-pipes, of which they made vigorous and unceasing use. I had not long to wait before a haggard old dame came up to where I stood and offered me her pipe for a smoke. When I accepted the courtesy, she went on to ask for my cigar, from which she took one or two hearty pulls, and then her face disappeared in a compound series of wrinkles, denoting delight at the unusual piquancy of the weed. After this the cigar was passed from mouth to mouth through the crowd, and carefully returned to me when they had all had a pull."

Thomson found the Pepohoans peaceful, friendly and helpful. While their villages were rustic, he was impressed with the way in which they creatively used local natural resources, like bamboo, to create novel technologies for home and work.

He also praised their tolerance despite being hemmed in from the south by Chinese encroachment and from the north by cannibalistic tribes, who sometimes devoured entire villages.

After a rough, rat-infested night and increasingly panicked pleas from his Chinese assistant, who said that the northern cannibals had recently developed a taste for Han Chinese stew, Thomson and Maxwell decided they would return to the Chinese-controlled plains. To get down, they needed to pass through an extremely dangerous stretch of cannibal-controlled territory. Enlisting a posse of armed Pepohoans, they set out with great trepidation, but Thomson still insisted on stopping frequently to photograph the striking scenery. Disregarding his companions' concerns, he found it hard to conceive of such savagery in such tranquil wilderness. Also, he noted that the weapons the "savages" of the far northern interior carried were supplied to them by the Chinese, indicating a situation perhaps less threatening than local legend would indicate.

Finally arriving in a "safe" village, a shabby trading post where nervous Chinese suppliers sold goods to non-cannibalistic middlemen, Thomson was disappointed in the change of scenery. The village was puny, and the only shop had nothing on its dusty shelves. Desperate to develop his photo plates, Thomson needed a pan. Having no success at the shop, after much wrangling he was finally able to wrest a dirty teapot from a elderly woman, and raced back to his camp to get to work. In order to properly prepare his solution, he and his servant, Ahong, had to stay up all night boiling down the liquid, a tedious job at the best of times, made much worse on a cold night after a hike. Thomson complained about Ahong dozing off, but soon followed suit and the liquid boiled off until it burst in a ball of flame:

"Once the alcoholic fumes in passing off caught fire; then I heard a terrible shriek and started up to find the scared face of a savage old woman glaring close to mine. She must have been placed there to watch us, and she vanished instantly into the darkness whence she had appeared. Ahong, disturbed in his sleep, caught sight of the apparition and declared that it was the — well, never mind what! But he did not rest quite so comfortably after that incident. I am not prepared myself to say what the old witch could have been, or how she vanished. She certainly looked haggard, hideous and unearthly, and her flight, too, was sudden and noiseless."

Neither frightened man managed to drift off again, and Thomson reported that the solution came out practically perfect, needing only an improvised dash of Chinese vinegar. The next day he felt he "would have much rather laid down and slept" than diligently photograph the sights of Formosa. Exhausted – but satisfied with his hard-won photos – Thomson headed back to the mainland.

He landed in Fukien Province and traveled up the Min River, the major river of the province and an important route for transporting tea. The scenery was quite a contrast to the mountains of Formosa. At the first port, he found the industrial landscape reminded him more of the smoggy line of factories along the River Clyde in Glasgow than the misty green hills of southern China. He found his next stop, the city of Foo-chow (Fuzhou), slightly more fetching, though his opinion of the place soured at the sight of the foreign concession. Deciding that the local cemetery was the most desirable plot of land in town, European investors had bought up tracts of ancient Foo-chow family tombs and planted their houses among them, which Thomson found exceedingly tasteless.

He then noticed a second "city of the dead" in Foo-chow, that of the impoverished. He detailed the squalor of their living conditions – some being so poor that inhabitants lived in the local mortuary, sharing beds with corpses –as well as the extortion they suffered at the hands of both the police and "beggar chiefs", and the horrible diseases they contracted and were unable to have treated (the local charity hospital had been taken over by an unscrupulous character and the patients were forced to work for him). Depressed, Thomson went on a spiritual retreat with a friend at a nearby monastery, which only augmented his frustration and disillusionment. Touched by the daily prayer ceremonies at the temple, he tried to enquire further about their significance, only to learn that the young monks did not even know the meanings of the prayers; they were just chanting the sounds from memory.

Thomson's next stop was Shanghai. His arrival was most inauspicious – his steamship mowed over a junk though fortunately the crew survived. Then Thomson was off to explore the foreign settlement.

He had heard much of Shanghai, noting:

"Shanghai has always been able to hold its own as the great Chinese emporium of foreign trade. It was therefore with feelings of profound interest that I for the first time beheld the splendid foreign settlement that stands there on the banks of the Wong-poo, at a spot which about sixty years ago was a mere swamp dotted with a few fisher huts, and inhabited by a miserable semi-aquatic sort of Chinese population."

From a distance, he was pleasantly surprised by the skyline of the foreign settlement – it reminded him of a quaint European seaport. And, upon closer inspection, he found it solidly constructed:

"What surprised me most about this settlement was the absence of anything temporary or unfinished in the style of its buildings, such as might remind one that the place was, after all, nothing more than a trading depot, planted on hostile and inhospitable shores, and sustained in its position in spite of the envy which its appearance excited among the rulers of the land."

He went on to contrast it with the "niggardliness and grinding despotism" of the Chinese quarter of the city. He saw this as a perfect illustration of the positive impact foreign powers could have, building prosperous cities out of backward Chinese slums. Toning down his cultural chauvinism, he also made a point of conceding that none of the splendid edifices in the foreign concessions could have been built without the skilled labor of local Chinese craftsmen, evidence that the "natives" could "evolve" as well.

One stormy night, after taking in his fill of Shanghai's society and scenery, Thomson boarded a steamer heading up the Yangtze River and began the arduous journey inland to Sichuan Province. The steamer could only take him as far as Hankow, after which the river was too difficult to navigate for heavy craft, so he hitched a ride with two Americans traveling in a native junk. The new craft may have been tiny and rickety, but it proved surprisingly nimble in navigating the rock-strewn rapids that peppered the Yangtze gorges. The scenery was, for Thomson, disappointingly un-photogenic (cliffs followed by more cliffs), but life on board kept him entertained. The captain's wife, Mrs. Wang, kept the captain and the surly crew in line, soon becoming the focal point of the trip:

"This difficulty [rousing the crew each morning] the gentle wife settled ultimately by kicking her husband out of bed on to the deck, hurling torrents of abuse at his unhappy head and supplementing those delicate attentions by a plentiful supply of cooking utensils. Let the reader imagine himself afloat in such a vessel as I have described, with such a crew, on a river red like the soil through which it flows, and from half a mile to a league in breadth; let him conceive himself ascending the stream between low level monotonous clay walls; he will then have a picture of our craft and our surroundings for many days as we pursued our voyage up to the Gorges."

Occasionally, the boat stopped and the travelers could have a quick ramble around the area. Most of the villages Thomson found to be painfully impoverished and isolated – none had ever seen a European, let alone a camera. At one town, he was swarmed by curious locals trying to figure out what sort of creature he was:

"All made numerous good-natured enquiries about our relations and our clothes; one old man even suggested that our faces and hands had only acquired a pale color through the use of some wonderful cosmetic, and that our bodies were black. I bared my arm to refute this calumny, and its white skin was touched by many a rough finger, and awoke universal admiration. Not knowing exactly what our barbarous views of decency might be, we were kindly recommended by an unwashed, but polished member of the community not to gratify vulgar curiosity by stripping entirely, as we had already completely satisfied the more intelligent members of the crowd."

Though he found the encounter entertaining, Thomson began to ruminate more thoughtfully on the widespread ignorance and "depraved notions" of Westerners in China. He complained that even the "merest coolie" felt that Westerners needed to be educated about China and would "readily place his knowledge at our service and put us in the way of picking up something of Chinese civilization", but then felt no need to reciprocate by seriously studying the West. While conceding that he might gain something from these generously shared lessons on Chinese culture, Thomson was miffed by the reciprocal apathy towards the Western world. Most Chinese seemed satisfied with wildly exaggerated tales (that some Europeans were clawed and preferred to hop on one foot than walk) rather than the "Enlightened truth."

At the foreign treaty river port of Ichang (today spelled Yichang), the river became too narrow for even their diminutive craft, so Thomson and his two American friends left the Wangs to their domestic disputes, venturing on in an even smaller boat through the murky and cavernous stretches of the gorges.

"The further we entered the gorges the more desolate and dark became the scene; the narrow barren defile presenting a striking contrast to the wide cultivated plains through which we had been making our way from the sea, for more than 1,000 miles."

Finding a link with home, the gloomy, "smoke begrimed" cave dwellings common in this area reminded him of ancient fishermen's huts on the north coast of Scotland; depressing abodes built with incredible amounts of industry and hope by pre-modern men. Again evidence, if Thomson needed any more, that the Chinese could modernize, just as the ancient Scottish fishermen had.

Deciding to examine this landscape and its "pre-modern" people more closely, Thomson asked for leave to walk along the shore for a short distance. Along the way, he ran into the local mandarin, who quizzed him on his strange "apparatus":

"While I was engaged in photographing the scene, I fell in with a mandarin, who asked many questions about my honorable name and title, my country, my kinsmen, and as he had never set eyes on a photographic instrument before, he wanted to see the result of my work. When the picture was shown to him, he enquired by what possible means a drawing could be so perfectly completed in so short a space of time; and then, without waiting for an answer, and casting an anxious glance at me to make sure I had neither horns, hoofs, nor tail visible, he hurried off to the village, with the conviction that my art was an uncanny one, and that my diabolical insignia were only craftily concealed."

The consequences of the encounter were later tangible, when a mob of angry villagers attacked him with clods of earth and stones. Running for his life, Thomson only barely escaped, after diving awkwardly into the river and swimming for the ship. On top of the near-lynching, a nasty scare with pirates and nearly crashing in the rapids, the addition of foul weather convinced Thomson and his two American friends that it was time to pack it in, and so – after making it all the way to Szechuan – the boat turned back for Shanghai.

On the way back down-river, they stopped off at Nanking (today spelled Nanjing), the walled city that had been the capital of the early Ming Dynasty which was not yet open to foreign trade. Thomson was hoping that here, finally, he would have a chance to glimpse the great architectural splendor that China was famed for, unblighted by grinding poverty and decay. But his travel was delayed and, when he arrived, he had no time to seek out accommodation, let alone see the sights. Having little choice, he decided to rough it in a shed near the steamer terminal, hoping to get some sleep for the morning's adventures. This proved to be a remarkably fortuitous turn of events. The crowded hut was buzzing with the news of the death of General Tseng-kuo-fan, a Taiping rebellion hero and a man Thomson was supposed to photograph while in town. Had he not been delayed and actually had the photo session that day, Thomson almost certainly would have been blamed for the general's demise, and possibly even tried for murder. Although he had not brought his camera near the man, he still needed to lay low while in Nanking and reign in his ambitious plans for photographing the city's architectural wonders.

93

Thomson ruminated on superstitions about photography both in China and in Britain:

"It is a wide-spread Chinese belief, from which men of intelligence are by no means free, that in taking a photograph, a certain portion of the vital principle is extracted from the body of the sitter, and that thus his decease within a limited period is rendered an absolute certainty. The reader will gather from this that I was frequently looked upon as a forerunner of death, as a sort of Nemesis in fact; and I have seen unfortunates, stricken with superstitious dread, fall down on bended knees and beseech me not to take their likeness or their life with the fatal lens of my camera. But all this might have occurred in our own country not many years ago, where a photograph would have been esteemed a work of the devil."

The scenery was not what he had hoped for either. Even the city's fabled porcelain tower, once one of the Seven Wonders of the World, had been leveled and was being sold off, brick by brick. Hoping for a better subject, Thomson set out for Peking.

After a tiring journey by boat, cart and foot, Thomson was in a bruised and disheveled state when he arrived in Peking. He found the famed city gates of the city to be no better, nothing more than "interesting relics of a bygone age." They were crumbling, their guard towers housed decoy wooden weapons rather than real canons, and the moats were little more than shallow, weed-infested lagoons. But once through the gates, things began to pick up.

"Highly picturesque and interesting," noted Thomson, a city waiting to be photographed. Its contrasts impressed him: thriving commerce and imperial excess mixed with bone-cracking poverty. The buildings themselves were "attractive", but Thomson's eye was drawn to the vibrant activity, especially on the streets. Here were impromptu markets where "everything under the Chinese sun" could be obtained, streaming crowds, ad-hoc architecture and imperial parades all jockeying for space. The view (and even the arrangement of the buildings!) shifted at whirlwind pace. At one point, Thomson attempted to photograph a busy street scene from a temporary wooden bridge, and found the planks beneath his feet shifting at a speed beyond his comprehension:

"Once, as I threaded my way along, I had to climb a pile of wooden planks to reach the path beyond, and finding that a clear view could be obtained from the top of a fine shop on the other side of the road, I had my camera set up and proceeded to take a photograph. But in two or three minutes, before the picture could be secured, there was a sudden transformation of the scene. Every available spot of ground was taken up by eager but good-natured spectators; traffic was suspended; and just as I was about to expose the plate, some ingenious youth displaced the plank on which I stood, and brought me down in a rapid, undignified descent, immensely entertaining to the crowd."

Among the chaotic activity, Thomson came upon trades not dissimilar to his own: stalls dealing in "magic pictures", foreign stereoscope photographs and even peep shows, though, he cautioned, "the less one says about them the better."

Besides his documentary work, Thomson produced his most important Chinese portrait commission in Peking, photographing the members of the Tsungli Yamen, or Chinese Foreign Office, in the intimate surrounds of their exclusive courtyard compound. These men were among the highest-ranking government officials and to meet them, let alone photograph them, was a great honor. Thomson proved equal to the task, taking several splendid photographs and discussing with them their positions on domestic and international policy.

Showing himself to be quite well informed about contemporary Chinese politics, he was particularly glad to meet the head of the office, Prince Gong, a famous advocate of stronger ties with the West. As he commented afterwards, the encounter left him awed by the scope of Gong's power, but also deeply concerned about the apparent ease with which he seemed to carry his heavy responsibilities:

"As I looked upon him, I wondered whether he felt the burden of the responsibility which he shared with the ministers around, in guiding the destinies of so many millions of the human race; or whether he and his distinguished colleagues were able to look with complacency upon the present state of the Empire and its people."

Thomson met a man In Peking, who made a lasting impression on him: Mr. Yang, a member of the intelligentsia, an inventor and amateur photographer.

"Yang was a fine sample of the modern Chinese savant — fat, good-natured and contented; but much inclined to take short cuts to scientific knowledge, and to esteem his own incomplete and haphazard achievements the results of marvelously perfect intelligence."

Despite his condescension, Thomson and Yang got on swimmingly, and he spent much of his Peking stop in Yang's workshop, fiddling with the latter's latest inventions. These visits also afforded Thomson his only glimpse into life inside a Peking courtyard. Though it "was tastefully laid out with rockeries, flowers, fish-ponds, bridges and pavilions", it was also scattered with new-fangled innovations like a steam-powered sawmill in the chicken coop, a dark room, and a chemistry lab in one of the lady's bedrooms. Yang was also in the process of installing gas-powered lighting ("a feat which I believe he successfully accomplished without blowing up his abode"). Thomson taught Yang how to develop his photos more effectively and Yang introduced Thomson to his family, including his wives, who were some of the only women Thomson met in Peking, and gave him entertaining lessons on Chinese culture.

Thomson purchased a little pony and spent the balance of his time sightseeing, finding Peking to be a photographer's paradise. He was astounded by the exactitude of Peking's careful symmetry. One of the world's first planned cities, Peking's streets were aligned in an exact grid, with the emperor's palace placed squarely in the center and key temples carefully situated in auspicious positions around it. When granted a bird's eye view from the walls, however, he was disappointed by what he found:

"Viewed from any stand-point on the outer wall, the whole scene is disappointing... the eye wearies of its wanderings over hundreds of acres of tiles and walls all of one stereotyped pattern."

Nonetheless, at the major sites in the city, he found more than enough picturesque material. He was particularly impressed by the Confucian temple ("perhaps the most imposing specimen of purely Chinese architecture to be found among the ornaments of the capital"), the National University (with its impressive stele inscribed with the classics), and the Observatory, where many of the instruments were provided by Jesuit missionaries in the 17th century.

Thomson capped his Peking sightseeing with a trip a few miles out of town to the former Summer Palace (Yuanming Yuan), which had recently been laid to waste by foreign troops at the end of the Second Opium War.

"There we found a wilderness of ruin and devastation which it was piteous to behold. Marble slabs and sculptured ornaments that had graced one of the finest scenes in China, now lay scattered everywhere among the debris and weeds."

Trying to inject some optimism into his account, he noted that the few remaining structures – a marble bridge and a temple –

were both quite fetching.

"Enough yet remained, however, to give some faint notion of the untold wealth and labor that must have been lavished on this Imperial retreat."

Such remains also made it evident just how lovely a place had been destroyed for purely political reasons, and he condemned foreign troops for using such methods in their attack. Perhaps naively, he suggested that in the future, rather than destroying places of such outstanding cultural value, foreign powers should instead simply impose a "wise and liberal administration" in the city, believing this would be sufficient to win over the people and deter the government.

Still shaken by the Summer Palace, Thomson left Peking in a somber mood, but not before visiting his final, northernmost destination, the Great Wall. He complained frequently that the journey was a rough one – the inns and roads were poor and the people were mean. He was exhausted both physically and mentally by the time he arrived, and he found the wall failed to meet his expectations.

"The Wall has often been described, but I confess that it disappointed me. It is simply a gigantic, useless stone fence, climbing the hills and dipping down into the valleys...It was never much more than a clay mound even in its best parts, faced with sun-dried bricks, and in the passes, as at Pan-ta-ling, with stone. It now only stands as a colossal monument of misdirected human labor, and of the genius which the Chinese have ever displayed in raising costly barriers to shut out barbarians from Cathay."

It was on this note of despair, both for China and for himself, that Thomson concluded his travels. While he conceded he had seen examples of splendid cultural and historic wealth, it was the images of backwardness, waste, destruction and squalor that had made the deepest impression on him.

"The picture at best is a sad one; and although a ray of sunshine may brighten it here and there, yet, after all, the darkness that broods over the land becomes but the more palpable under this straggling, fitful light. Poverty and ignorance we have among us in England; but no poverty so wretched, no ignorance so intense as are found among the millions of China."

5

OSCAR TERRY CROSBY

TIBET & TURKESTAN

FOR SUCH AN ADVENTUROUS character, one who managed to push his way into the upper echelons of Great Game politics to feed his wanderlust, Oscar Terry Crosby (1861-1947) had a fairly unexceptional start in life.

He was born in the rural Louisiana town of Ponchatoula, truly a backwater. At the age of eighteen, he joined the US Military Academy at West Point and after graduation he married a hometown girl and dutifully served out a stint in the Army Corps of Engineers, where he specialized in the latest state-of-the-art technology, electricity. He resigned his commission a few years later for a more lucrative and stable career in the burgeoning electricity industry, and achieved the modest distinction of being appointed president of the Potomac Power Company in Washington D.C. in 1896, at the age of 35.

Despite his professional successes, Crosby was not content. In 1900, he abruptly switched gears, left behind his lucrative yet humdrum corporate career in exchange for an adventure tour in Africa. Traveling extensively through Abyssinia (present-day Ethiopia) and Sudan, he was thrilled by the exotic scenery and his frequent run-ins with danger, proving himself to be fearless and inquisitive. His technical military training also proved valuable in terms of extracting himself from various scrapes. By the end of the trip, he no longer considered himself to be an amateur traveler, but an explorer.

Upon his return to the US, Crosby quickly ingratiated himself with the various anthropological and geographical societies of his day, becoming a frequent and enthusiastic lecturer. And in 1903, he headed out on another adventure, this time to Tibet and Turkestan in 1903, and again in 1913 for an extensive tour of the Middle East and Asia. Both adventures resulted in the collection of priceless artifacts and manuscripts, all of which he conscientiously donated to libraries and museums in the United States. Some of his finds are still being researched by historians, anthropologists and linguists today. By 1909, after the publication of his travelogue Tibet and Turkestan, he was considered to have accumulated such expertise on Asian affairs that he was selected as a candidate for the post of China Minister by the US government, though he was ultimately not selected.

The onset of World War I seemed likely to curb his travels, but Crosby, with his extensive administrative experience in the power industry, was able to secure a post as the director of the Commission for the Relief of Belgium in 1915, allowing travels to Belgium and Northern France. He became increasingly well connected in political circles and by 1917 he was appointed Assistant Secretary of the Treasury in the US, and president of the Inter-Ally Council on War Purchases and Finance. At the end of the war, he was named "United States Special Commissioner of Finance in Europe", making him the American government's go-to for decisions on post-war reparations, and putting him in close contact with major European public figures like John Maynard Keynes and Austen Chamberlain. While he proved skilled at international power politics, his encounters with war-torn Europe deeply troubled him, and he soon re-focused his career once again. This time he decided to use his political clout to push for world peace.

Working closely with other high-profile peace campaigners, among them US president Woodrow Wilson, Crosby published a book on the subject, International War, Its Causes and Its Cure. *The book had limited success, but was among the first to question heavy German reparations (of which he had partly been the architect), presciently considering them to be a potential catalyst for future conflict.*

In the mid-1920s, Crosby finally retired from public service and returned to adventuring. He went on two more major expeditions to Africa, covering wide swathes of territory in Namibia, Tanganyika, Kenya and the Belgian Congo, and collecting more colorful stories and artifacts along the way. His final trip was more subdued: in 1937, he took a tour of northern Europe (Germany, Poland, Russia and Romania), only to witness the peace he had campaigned so energetically for dissolving into the Second World War. Crosby died in 1947, living just long enough to see the foundations of a second attempt at post-war peace take shape.

In Tibet and Turkestan, Crosby takes his readers through his death-defying 1903 adventures on the caravan routes of Turkestan (present day Uzbekistan, Kyrgyzstan, Kazakhstan and Xinjiang) and the nomad trails of the hostile Tibetan plateau. He immodestly considers himself the first independent observer in this region of the world, dismissing out-of-hand the "biased" reports of previous Western explorers:

"I feel myself fortunate in that no official obligation of any kind burdens me in the expression of the opinions that have arisen from such direct observation and subsequent study as I have made. It is, I believe, true that all others who have visited these secluded regions in recent years are more or less embarrassed by some official or personal ties."

His book is peppered with liberal and forthright commentary

that seeks to inform both amateurs and experts on this region previously "known only vaguely, except to certain officials who can speak only in accord with the policies they serve." Though many of his comments are insightful and his projections about the future of the region remarkably accurate, he does at times get carried away in his role as an "impartial outsider". Some of his (certainly "independent") predictions for Turkestan and Tibet could best be described as flights of fancy, like his anticipation of a "peaceful" Russian Revolution, a calm affair to be lead by cultured and unruffled administrators in Russian Turkestan.

Intending to take on the wilds of Turkestan and Tibet by himself, Crosby made his own way from Washington D.C. to his expedition's starting point on the Caspian Sea. Before setting off, however, he fell in with a friendly French Army captain, Fernand Anginieur, who decided he would like to join the adventure. Crosby acquiesced, so after telegraphing to request leave from his commanding officer (one imagines it must have been open-ended), Anginieur collected his things and "cast in his lot" with Crosby.

Crosby and Anginieur formed a tight bond from day one, with Crosby even sappily writing:

"I wish more of my compatriots could meet and know such Frenchmen as are typified in Anginieur. 'Brilliant but superficial and frivolous' is a hasty judgement which one often hears from English-speaking critics of the French. 'Brilliant, loyal, and earnest' – such is the type whom one finds in making the acquaintance of my friend Anginieur."

Later on, when the going got rough, Anginieur would prove himself to be a fortuitous addition to the team.

The two men set off from Krasnovodsk on the shores of Caspian Sea, transported for the first leg of the journey in a private railway car specially arranged by the Russian Railway

Minister with amenities like a formal sitting room, full bathroom and shower, and a personal servant. The only other member of the party – their polyglot interpreter, Joseph – was relegated to second class, even though "he [was] a neat person and [didn't] look rumpled in the mornings."

After a few days, the team arrived at their first stop in Turkestan proper, Bokhara (in present-day Uzbekistan), a city famed for the architectural beauty of its eighty mosques. Leaving the boring, modern Russian quarter behind (its only point of interest being the train station they had arrived in), they struck out for the "animated tunnels" of the exotic Silk Road bazaars in the "native city".

"You enter [the bazaar] by way of melons; you progress through brass-work, iron-mongery, saddlery, butchery, cookery; then the appetising fumes from open-air restaurants may float temptations in half-a-dozen directions. Near by are sweet-meats, then brilliant skullcaps, then European calicos, then true, fascinating Bokhara silks…"

Their next stop, Samarcand, captured their imaginations with its colorful history as the fourteenth century cultural capital of Tamerlane and a conquest of both Alexander the Great and Genghis Khan. Crosby was enthralled by the "great mosques and tombs whose white-and-blue beauty it is so hard to suggest in words", being particularly touched by an ornate mosque built by Tamerlane in honor of his consort Bibi Khanim. He considered it a monument to love on a par with the Taj Mahal and, after noting that both were built to honor spouses of polygamous husbands, pondered the possible benefits of such a marriage arrangement, noting, "We of European condition have been made to develop much monogamy with responsibilities, and some polygamy without responsibilities. Asia and Africa have been made to develop much polygamy, some monogamy, and some polyandry, all with responsibility. There is plainly a difference of social adaptability – as there are difference of flora and fauna. Let us cease to curse our divergent neighbour – let us try to feel that all trees and all men and all relations of things have been made by the same power and that they constantly obey it."

Leaving the beauty of Samarcand behind, the pair of adventurers popped over to the adjoining Russian quarter, where they were entertained by General Madinsky. Bored with the quiet life of the Russian frontier, the general was happy for the company and even gave Crosby a loaded Smith and Wesson pistol as a token of his affection – he had no need for it in dull, tranquil Samarcand anyway. Crosby was fascinated by Russian frontiersmen such as this, administrators and military men who lived out their lives in the distant corners of the empire, speaking fluent French and dancing fashionable St. Petersburg reels, but never traveling west of the Urals. They reminded him of American pioneers with their self-reliance, sense of adventure and gift for recreating a version of "home" in a distant land.

From his encounters with Madinsky and men of his ilk, Crosby foresaw the makings of a low-key Russian revolution: a peaceful and safe transfer of power from the oligarchy to a democratically elected government, to be lead by these well-heeled emissaries posted in far-flung Russian outposts. As he described it: "I see nothing to suggest destruction of the essential unity of the Empire, or any cataclysmic change in its form." It was a far cry from the violent movements that would soon take place in 1907 and 1917.

After Samarcand, the private carriage took them to Kokand, where there were "no monuments to beguile us," but there was a decent dry goods store. Their translator dismissed the stock, claiming supplies were much better further along at the garrison town of Osh – about thirty miles beyond the terminus of the railway, and the point from which they would start their caravan travel to Kashgar, the capital of Chinese Turkestan – so they hopped back aboard the train and headed to the end of the line.

They disembarked definitively where the tracks dead-ended into the wastelands of earthquake shattered Andijan. Three years earlier, over 10,000 people had been "snuffed out" here by a massive quake, and the town now was nothing more than a ruin. There were scattered signs that things were picking up, like religious gatherings in the roofless mosques and churches, but the overall picture was grim and the party quickly pushed on to Osh. Traveling off the rails for the first time, Crosby and Anginieur found the journey (a rough ride through the desert) more taxing. The weather was scorching and, without their personal servant, the food was foul. Of the Russian chef at the only road-side eatery along the way, Crosby remarked:

"That he can make chai is incontestable. An all-comprehending soup he also makes. As to anything else, we prefer simple fare rather than watch his sloppy preparations. The stable is very near, the flies are nearer, the smells are nearest, and the man's methods are dirty."

But they cheered themselves with the thought of Osh's rich supplies and set out again.

But Osh was a disappointment. Rather than well-stocked stores, they found moldy groceries and countless administrative hurdles. Armed with the same letter of introduction from the Minister of Foreign Affairs in St. Petersburg that had scored them the private rail carriage, Crosby and Anginieur had expected all doors to be open as they prepared their caravan to travel the 250 miles from Osh to Kashgar. Instead, they were coldly informed that they had neglected to obtain exit permits for the Russo-Sino frontier from the provincial government, and getting them would involve backtracking and weeks of delay. They were made to feel distinctly unwelcome.

Much diplomatic wrangling ensued, and many eyebrows were raised at Anginieur's story that he had decided "on the spur of the moment" to join the expedition, but eventually the needed permits were obtained and supplies – though mediocre – were purchased. Anxious to get out of town before further "issues" cropped up, Crosby decided he wouldn't hang around to wait for his special chronometer, being shipped to him from St. Petersburg, and made arrangements with the cook-cum-postmaster to forward it to him in Kashgar. This proved a big mistake, as Crosby admitted: "Just why a man of some experience in travel should commit such folly I know not. A few months later there was full and fair punishment for my error."

They carried on in high spirits through the desert heat to Kashgar.

"The road was dusty, and it was hot, because Central Asia in July is always hot. But our mounts were fairly good; the country was green all about us through the twenty-five mile strip of irrigation; the people were interested and interesting."

There wasn't much to see – just a handful of homesick Russian telegraph operators and some Kirghiz herders. The Russo-Sino frontier was fairly unremarkable, lost as it was in the Turkestan deserts, though Crosby reflected poetically on the humble meeting point of the two great empires:

"The simple Cossack officer, with whom we ate black bread three days ago, was commissioned by [the Tsar], a magic-worshipping, devout Christian tyrant in St. Petersburg. This courteous yellow man, whose ragged soldiers light the way with lanterns, lives by the breath of an old woman [the Empress Dowager] who guesses at outside things from Pekin's thick-shadowed imperial garden."

Twelve days after setting out, Crosby and Anginieur arrived

in Kashgar. It was a charming, welcoming city, one of "narrow bazaars, defenceless gates and blind alleys". Letter of invitation in hand, they headed for the Russian Consulate where, Crosby had been informed by a Petersburg diplomat some months earlier, they would be warmly welcomed and provided with comfortable lodgings. Unfortunately, communications between Kashgar and St. Petersburg must have been out of synch, as there was not a bed to spare, and the Russians quickly offloaded them onto the British envoy, Captain Miles. The affable Miles had no actual diplomatic power in the region, his clunky title of "Temporary Assistant to the Resident at Srinagar for Chinese Affairs" merely indicated that he was the powerless underling of an equally powerless regional governor based twenty days travel away. He couldn't help them arrange any of the various stamps required by the Chinese authorities for their onward travel, but he did help organize their accommodations and caravan.

But they were fortunate to have Miles on their side, because at this point Joseph decided that life on the road was simply too much and headed back for a summer of relaxation by the Caspian Sea. Miles quickly rustled up a new translator, Achbar. His interpretation skills were limited ("his vocabulary was painfully extended from twenty-five to fifty words, and one blank stare"), but he was the only one in town and they were relieved to have him. The rest of the team included Mir Mullah (an experienced but elderly Afghan mountaineer), Lassoo (a faithful and steadfast Ladaki) and Mohammed Joo (a sturdy Kashmiri horse trader).

During their sojourn in Kashgar, the team became increasingly aware of the Chinese presence. Though there was only a small population of Han Chinese living in Kashgar, the Taotai (regional governor appointed by Peking) wielded impressive power. There was no doubt that the government in Peking was aware of the territorial significance of this region bordering both Russian

Turkestan and British-controlled Kashmir. Crosby discovered during his stay that the Chinese central government had secretly built a telegraph wire connecting Peking and Kashgar, covering a distance of more than two thousand miles, in order to keep better tabs on the region.

The party's own audience with the Taotai hinted that Peking was equally concerned about American and French "explorers" making claims on the region as they were about the British and Russians, and Crosby's requests for letters of introduction for Khotan and Polu (the next two towns on their Turkestan itinerary) were brushed aside. The Russian consulate, Mr. Petrovsky, proved equally wily, insinuating that they were hiding the true nature of their expedition and refusing letters of introduction. Crosby, while disappointed, understood the politics at hand.

"It appears as plain as a pikestaff that vagrant French and Americans should not be encouraged to spy out the land and perhaps to create incidents out of which new ideas might be born. Would Cortez have welcomed independent English or French travelers in Mexico while he was preaching to wondering Aztecs the doctrine of his master's universal dominion?"

Even more frankly, he admitted that he and Anginieur were indeed keeping secrets, just as the Russians and Chinese suspected; they had decided not to reveal that their final aim was Lhasa, instead asking only for permission to travel to the eastern Turkestan towns of Khotan and Polu on their way to Ladak (a Tibetan province that had been recently annexed by Kashmir), fearing any mention of Tibet would bring rejection out of hand.

After days of posturing, the adventurers were finally granted permission to proceed. Their send-off party mirrored the political situation, with the delicate and ever discreet Peking-appointed mayor, the belligerent guard of the Cossacks, mild-mannered Miles and a feisty Dutch missionary, Father Hendricks, all coming to say their goodbyes. Letting bygones be bygones, Crosby said:

"Our parting was the parting of men who liked each other – of mutually helpful beings thrown together, thrown apart, by the Power which made your eyes brown or blue and your faith whatever it may be."

Father Hendricks was a seasoned and well-connected China-hand (he had spent decades in Mongolia and Turkestan) and a fervent Russophobe (he held a mysterious belief that the Bible named the Russians as an evil race) and decided, on the spur of the moment, to accompany them as far as Khotan to prevent any further diplomatic shenanigans. Despite Hendricks' paranoia, life on the road to Khotan was one of camaraderie and leisure, with the men engaging in energetic debates on the meaning of life as they meandered through the desert. Though the growing Russian and British influence brought ever more European products to the region, there was not a single European resident east of Kashgar, and Hindu traders were the only other foreigners around. Without Father Hendricks' assistance, which was much more effective than Achbar's half-hearted translations, Crosby and Anginieur would have had a much rougher ride.

Arriving in Khotan, they were warmly welcomed by a guard of honor composed of the town's expat Hindu population. These Hindu traders hosted them lavishly, providing deluxe accommodation and an abundance of food. They found Khotan was "a [mud-walled] maze of alleys, paths, streets" whose ancient structures impressed them with their history. Crosby and Anginieur tried their luck in the bazaar, where they were pleased to find cheap hand-made carpets and scraps of antique manuscripts, which had survived for thousands of years buried in the sands of the desert, remnants of ancient societies long since disappeared.

"Thus we see the desert as destroyer [of the civilization which created the scripts], the desert as preserver, but as preserver only of the empty husks of that life which for a season was permitted to flourish."

An Andijani in the employ of the Russians tried to muscle in and "take them under his wing", but the vigilant Hendricks spurned his advances and "moving on the very ragged edge of policy" determined that he himself would see to the rest of their arrangements, including getting yet another set of stamps and letters from the local governor.

The Chinese officials in Khotan proved to be friendlier and less suspicious than they had been in Kashgar. They warned the party to avoid heading to Tibet, seemingly out of genuine concern for their safety rather than to keep Tibet under wraps. Taking advantage of the fact that these officials "advised, but did not command", Crosby and party set off quickly (before any messengers from Kashgar arrived to spoil things).

A few miles outside of Khotan, they bid Hendricks farewell, "and then we were away to struggle with the desert, the mountain, the deathly cold, and with Achbar." Their lives depend on the "marshalling together of about fifty words over the empty parade ground of [Achbar's] mind", but they reached their final staging post, Polu, a week later, unscathed. There they rushed through the final preparations for the Tibetan steppe, fearing the onset of winter and desperate to conceal their true destination. Unexpectedly, the local people told them that another white man had arrived in town. This was indeed curious, since only a handful of hardy (or lost) Europeans had made it to Polu before them, so they went over to make their introductions. It turned out that the man was an itinerant Siberian who made his living with a graphophone show, entertaining rural Turkestani tribes with recordings of the Russian, French and English languages.

Remembering Hendricks' warnings, Anginieur and Crosby

wondered whether this was a Russian spy sent to tail them, but his outfit seemed so ludicrous, they decided it might just be genuine. Later treachery in Tibet lead them to recall the strange man, though Crosby also dryly offered another, more obvious, explanation for the appearance of duplicity: "We dealt through the unspeakable Achbar. There was room for some misunderstanding."

The next day they set off on their secret adventure, which they intended to be a two-week journey towards the Tibetan town of Rudok followed by a ride to Lhasa (rather than their stated destination of Ladak in Kashmir). Though the climb was steep, their eight men, sixteen donkey handlers and three servants did admirable work, fording rivers, making good time and coping with freezing temperatures. Three days into the journey, the team members began to quit one by one and headed back to town. Frustrated (and unable to source new men), Crosby and Anginieur offered hefty sums to the remaining handlers if they agreed to stick it out to the end of the trip.

The next stage of the journey was a steep four-day climb up a pass leading to the Tibetan plateau; Crosby and Anginieur needed to ride ahead with a forward party to ensure the trail was safe, while the handlers trailed a day or so behind. After reaching the top, the exhausted forward party spent several days convalescing and adjusting to the altitude. It turned out to be a pleasant time – they hunted game, drank endless cups of tea and set up camp. After a while, they began to get anxious for the rest of the team, of which there had been no sign. Supply rations were tight and the handlers were carrying most of them, so they couldn't afford to waste more time lounging around at the top of the trail. A search party was sent back down the path and returned with terrible news: the remainder of the team had fled with the donkeys, pitching the grain and supplies down a canyon. Just enough was recovered that, provided they reached Rudok within fifteen days, the party would survive, but there was no longer any room for error. Believing that things were under control, Crosby and Anginieur decided to carry on. It was at this point that the guide began to get cold feet, feigning illness and claiming he needed to return to the village. Smelling a rat, they ordered him bound day and night to Mir Mullah and doubled his wages. Nonetheless, he managed to escape his shackles and, taking no more than a crust of bread, hiked back to Polu on foot.

Thus they found themselves without a guide or even a reliable map in a barren valley on the Tibetan plateau. Crosby's chronometer, which would easily have allowed them to navigate the plains, had never made it beyond the sloppy Russian postmaster near Osh, and his second resort, a nautical atlas, which could have helped him place their latitude, had been stolen. With nothing more than an inaccurate compass, they decided to forge ahead. They knew the approximate direction to head (southwest) and their alternatives were limited.

Leaving the valley where the double-crossing guide had deposited them was backbreaking work – several of the ponies almost broke their necks slipping down the rock face – but their troubles were only just beginning. They unknowingly turned off from the road to Rudok almost as soon as they had begun and wandered off into dangerous uncharted territory in the Akasi Chin (White Desert).

"We had convinced ourselves that we could identify certain ranges as shown on the meagre maps, and for a few days we actually saw, at about five-miles intervals, artificial heaps of stone, probably marking some native trail of rarest use, from Polu to the salt lakes or to Rudok."

After a few days, the ponies began to die from altitude sickness. Shortly thereafter, they found themselves without water and Crosby nearly died chasing mirages in hopes of finding a stream.

"Life was but a constant strain of search for water, for fuel of roots or dung, for a bit of grazing, and always for a trail that never was found, because it had never been."

The fate cut them some slack and they came across a large fresh water lake where a day was spent a day recuperating, but with winter approaching and limited supplies, they needed to get back on the right trail fast.

What lay ahead was a steep mountain range, which they were convinced needed to be crossed if they were ever to reach Rudok. Working from hearsay from the servants and guesswork based on the clumsy maps, they set forth with as much energy as they could muster in an attempt to find a navigable pass through the mountains. Their climb was made more challenging by the fact the servants constantly contradicted themselves, meaning the party scaled peaks only to descend them again, heading first south, then north. As supplies dwindled, they became desperate to find any trail at all – it didn't matter anymore whether it led to Rudok as long as it lead to civilization. Crosby and Anginieur clutched at every shred of advice the servants gave, no matter how confusing.

"Mohammed Joo, ever an optimist, said that was the Lanak Pass. Lassoo said it was not, but he could take us to Lanak and probably find shepherds there. Our hearts swelled with satisfaction. A shepherd meant a trail; a trail meant a way back to the world where people lived, where the map should no longer be blank!"

None of the advice proved correct.

Exhausted from their ramblings at such an altitude, Anginieur developed a severe fever and cold. With only a tiny cup of water and little medicine, Crosby did his best to administer to his

friend, but it became clear that the party would need to rest for
an entire day while he recovered, which meant further taxing the
dangerously underfed, overburdened and altitude-sick ponies.
Two ponies had to be shot – they no longer had enough grain to
feed them – and the Westerners had to leave behind two horse-
loads of supplies. Clothes, books, camp chairs and even the
sextant were ditched.

Back on the trail again, things got worse. The valley they
happened to be following, while at least containing a stream,
seemed to head back into the White Desert, so despite the
desperate pleas of their servants, who feared leaving the
water, Crosby and Anginieur decided to veer back towards the
mountains, which they were still convinced they needed to cross
to reach safety. The path lead so steeply uphill that three more
ponies died, and what they found when they reached the top
was sobering:

"We found ourselves on a mountaintop, the very abomination
of desolation. [We] looked at the world, and it was not good to
behold; magnificent, but not good. Vast snow-crowned heights,
like gigantic foam billows, met at every point a now threatening
sky. A deep valley looked up at us from the west, but visible issue
there was none. There was absolutely nothing to suggest a way
out of the wildly massed region of snow save death or retreat."

Admitting this was no way forward, the two men finally
acquiesced to their servants' demands and headed back for the
trickle of a stream in the valley, hoping that it would not lead
them back to certain death in the desert.

By the time they made it back to the stream, the situation was
even direr – they simply didn't have sufficient supplies for the
entire party to carry on. So, setting up camp (which they dubbed
"Camp Purgatory") in a grassy spot by the side of the stream,
they sent their two most trusted servants, Mohammed Joo and

Lassoo, to find help. Crosby, Anginieur, Achbar and Mir Mullah would have to wait, with enough food for 12 days of half-rations, and most likely no way out if the scouts failed to return.

Anginieur developed phlebitis, a painful paralysis in one of his legs, and was unable to even leave the tent. This added a new dimension to their panic:

"For the upkeeping of our courage, we had talked much and fallaciously about walking toward safety, when the ponies should all have died; scheming to use them inside of us when they could no longer bear us as burdens on their backs...When several days had passed, and our poor ministrations to the invalid leg were shown to be futile, there came a sort of resignation to our inactivity, a sort of restful finality concerning the impossibility of walking out of our trouble."

The approach of their death became real and Crosby noting darkly:

"A good dose of Mauser lead could at least shorten heartache and hunger pain."

Anginieur and Crosby then hit upon the idea of sending Mir Mullah ten miles away to "Camp Abandon" to fetch the books and tools they had dumped. Through Achbar's limited translation capacities, they gave instructions for all books to be carried back (and, optimistically, some shoes, in case they decided to walk it), and then waited anxiously for his return.

Return he did, though through some massive error in translation, rather than carrying the trunk packed with volumes of Kant, Spinoza and Descartes, the confused servant brought back their formal evening wear and a copy of the Bible. The agnostic Crosby was beside himself with disappointment, but tried his best to remain composed, "It was ungracious that one, even nominally a Christian, should curse a Mussulman for bringing him the Bible."

Crosby spent his days tending to Anginieur's leg and distracting him from his agony by reading out lengthy passages from the Bible. After six days, there was no sign of the scouts, and the food stocks were halfway depleted. Somewhat unfairly, considering the circumstances, Crosby and Anginieur claimed the remainder of the more nutritious tinned foods for themselves, leaving the servants rice and stale bread. They even complained bitterly when one Russian can yielded only pickled cabbage when they had expected meat.

Crows began to flock to the camp, a sign, the servants reported darkly, that they expected to soon be carrion fodder. Crosby tried to chase the birds away with stones, but in his weakened condition, he was no match for them. The next day, he reported, "three of our ponies, having nothing else to do had now died."

On the eleventh day of waiting, with only one set of rations left, Crosby staggered out onto the frozen stream with a rifle, desperate to get a fish, even if it meant blowing the ice out from under him. Taking shaky aim, he fired into the water with no success except to knock himself off balance. Soggy and disheartened, he believed he was suffering from delusions when his fire was matched by three shots from the hills below them. Fortunately for the starving team, this was no fantasy, but the scouts on their way back!

After over a week on the trail, they returned, well-fed with extra horses, plenty of food and a party of helpful Kirghiz nomads. After a hearty meal of mutton and clotted yak's cream, everyone was feeling better. The Kirghiz rode off to Camp Abandon, bringing back the much-missed volumes of French philosophy and the rest of the ditched baggage, and scouts filled the team in on their location: in the valley of the Karakash River, a waterway that led straight back to Turkestan instead of Tibet.

Despite their recent trials, Crosby wanted to travel with the

Kirghiz, still planning on heading to Rudok. Savvier about the local terrain, the Kirghiz would have none of it, unwilling to expend any more supplies on the motley expedition and their misguided mountain-crossing plans. The party had no choice but to follow the herders back to their yurts, where a local guide could lead them to the road to Ladak – ironically, their stated "destination" the whole time – and from there onwards to "civilization". Crosby was frustrated, though resigned.

"Man is essentially Unsatisfied Desire and an Irritated Sensibility. These people had come in the nick of time to save my life; their refusal to help me Rudokward was in every way reasonable, yet there was a moment of rebellious indignation. Soon, however, It-might-have-been was buried deep in It-is, and we turned toward thoughts of departure."

At the mercy of the Kirghiz, their revised route was decided: they were aiming for the railway in India. Although they had believed themselves at the ends of the earth, telegraph-connected Ladak was only 20 days away and the railway 20 more. As Crosby wryly put it:

"There should be some hardship still – the Karakoram route is not Rotten Row – but, barring such accidents as are always possible in crossing glaciers, snow masses, and narrow defiles, we might now consider ourselves at the railway station in Rawal Pindi, or in Paris, for that matter."

Once they arrived in the Kirghiz village, Crosby was delighted.

"They were dignified, yet respectful; they were poor, but honest; they were hospitable but not fawning; we were helpless in their power, and they sold their scant provisions and their labour [for fair prices]."

The Kirghiz gave them camels and guides, showed them how to cook unleavened bread and even got Anginieur's leg on the mend. After two leisurely days at camp, they were back on the road, heading for the main caravan route. The ten-day ride to the caravan path felt as isolated as their wanderings in the desert – they only passed one solitary yurt in the entire time – they were surprised to meet some rather cosmopolitan characters. One unruffled Kirghiz wife just shrugged at the sight of Crosby and Anginieur: she had seen Europeans before, this was no big deal.

"When, a few days later, we struck the main trail beaten by the foot-fall of the centuries, we felt that we were again suddenly caught in the whirl of life's currents. Now caravans were met – one, two, or three each day. Now we got tobacco and sugar; we even had news of a friend, the Hindoo Aksakol from Yarkand."

Though the road was well-travelled, it was still treacherous. Their climb up the Karakoram Pass was littered with the skeletons of animals, and perhaps their masters, who had not survived the journey. "Thus in regions uninhabitable, death remains the only evident monument of the transient life that ventures here."

At the top of the pass, they camped at the infamous trading point Camp Sasar. Here, at incredible altitudes and in the bitter chill of the Himalayan peaks, caravans from Kashmir would deposit bales of merchandise for traders from Turkestan to collect. Though it may have seemed risky, there was only one route through the mountains and the traders working it were few and well-connected, so any traveler carrying bundles not his own would likely meet an untimely end. Sasar may have seemed desolate, but tight strings of commerce and society bound it both to Kashmir and to Turkestan.

The next day, Crosby and Anginieur reached the peak of the pass, 18,000 feet above sea level, still a few days journey from the Tibetan villages of Ladak. Crosby described his view from this highest point of their travels:

"The vision that comes back to me is one of supernal clarity;

across it, here and there, a veil of snow-born, wind-driven mist; pressing through it, a line of small black figures, men and yaks and ponies, surging slowly forward to some end know only to [them]."

Perhaps even more touching than the vista from this extreme elevation was the sight of a tree – the first they had seen in over two months – which popped up around a bend in the trail a few days later. They arrived in the "green, gold and russet groves, yellowing fields of grain and men's houses [of the Nubra Valley]...A nobler sight one may not see than this Himalayan vale set against the far-shining snow-peaks from which the high gods look down to bless."

Though technically controlled by Kashmir, this was thoroughly Tibetan territory. Many of the monasteries had been recently emptied ny the Kashmiri authorities, but the population remained devout, with pilgrims still pressing on to Lhasa, red-robed monks roaming the villages and prayer flags in front of nearly every house. The valley was lush, the people prosperous and the food abundant.

The valley was entirely Tibetan in custom, but the pressures of the Kashmiri regime (pressured by British colonial rule) and the Chinese government, which proclaimed itself master of all Tibet, clearly manifested themselves. In one incident, Crosby and Anginieur were brought up short in a rural inn when they came across a missive directly from Buckingham Palace hanging on the grungy wall:

"So it came to pass that in Panamirgh, twenty marches distant from the nearest permanent British official, we came upon a proclamation of King Edward's enthronement, avouched in proper English. In such strange and outcast places do the antennae that radiate from London and Pekin now learn to touch each other, to irritate, withdraw, return, first at Leh, then Lhasa, then farther afield."

Leh (the capital of Ladak) brought contact with Westerners – the first they had seen since they left Father Hendricks in Khotan. A family of German missionaries had been proselytizing in the valley for over forty years with limited success. Crosby found them fairly pathetic, considering their paltry conversion register, but he kept his comments to himself. Leh finally brought telegraph contact and messages were sent home to reassure families in America and France. It also brought the breaking up of the party. Mir Mullah, Lassoo and Mohammed Joo, the brave servants who had suffered and stood by them during their darkest days on the road to Rudok, all headed back over the mountains to Turkestan. The ever-hopeless interpreter Achbar stuck with them until their arrival in Srinagar (in Kashmir proper), but from here on in they made little use of his wretched translations.

The final stretch of road, from Leh to Srinagar, was quite unlike the dangerous mountain passes they had covered earlier. Simple yet comfortable "dak bungalows" lined the road, providing suitable cover at night. The roads were smooth and well-traveled, the going easy. The human landscape began to shift as they approached Kashmir proper:

"For two or three days we are still in the country of the Tibet people: long, black, and dirty queues, three-cornered hats, rusty lama-gowns, fluttering prayers, graven stones, rude shrines in high places, eyrie monasteries, the scant, laborious fields rock-anchored on the steep hillside, huddled villages, the sinuous and sparkling Indus, the unattainable heights of the snow crowning the barren slopes. Then at a turn in the trail…we cantered on, out of Lamaism, and slept in another world, a pukka Mohammedan village."

Suddenly their fellow travellers were Muslim pilgrims on the Haj, rather than Tibetans returning from Lhasa. On his first night in a Kashmiri lodge, Crosby was woken by the wailing prayers of the Hajji, and, believing them to be in pain or danger, begged Achbar to help him inquire as to their trouble. Achbar's refusal was attributed, as usual, to his uselessness (although in this case he knew what he was doing), so Crosby persisted. He burst into their room in order to "rescue" them, and it wasn't until much face had been lost on all sides that it became clear that the pilgrims were merely praying.

In the next few days they covered a lot of ground, speeding past the pilgrims, snacking on fresh fruit and even chatting with a "gold-stockinged, English-speaking, joke-loving native Commissioner, fresh from Kipling's pages."

They had to cross one last pass, the Zoji, but at a lowly 12,000 feet it was nothing compared to what they had already encountered. Some newly-fallen snow made the way more difficult (they were the last to cross through that year), and they "had once more the joy-killing experience of discharging the animals and man-handling the loads." They gladly greeted the green plains of Kashmir once through.

"Are there not a few days in your memory which are garlanded for their beauty and are perfumed by their happiness? – the day you learned to swim, your wedding day…? Such a day comes to him who, breasting still the Himalayan snows, out from the Himalayan nakedness, rides down from Zoji Pass, viewing the glorious vestments of the Sind, where it rushes to sink on the fair bosom of the vale of Kashmir."

They were relieved, excited, and proud as some of the first Europeans to ever arrive in Kashmir via such a challenging route. The next morning brought them "sunshine, fresh eggs, good ponies, and light hearts". They continued on to Srinagar, the first town of any consequence since Kashgar, where they spent several days enjoying the sights and sounds; they were impressed in equal measure by Srinagar's exotic character and its healthy expat community.

"Hindoo ruins, mysteriously suggestive; a good hotel; plenty of white people, sahibs and mem-sahibs; golf grounds; shops overflowing with fascinating goods and oily smiles of merchants; splendid tree-lined avenues leading to the mountains... such is Srinagar."

Homesickness pulled them onwards. After bidding a final, unemotional farewell to Achbar, they set off for the "Outside". Their remaining travel was an easy route with smooth roads and speedy trains, so Crosby brought the narrative of their expedition to an abrupt close, directing his adventure-hungry readers elsewhere: "The Outside is, first, Rawal Pindi, which is on the railway, then all India lying before us. It is in the guidebooks and in Kipling. You may drink it as beer from the guidebooks or sip it as nectar from Kipling."

6

ELIZABETH KENDALL

A WAYFARER IN CHINA: IMPRESSIONS OF A TRIP ACROSS WEST CHINA AND MONGOLIA

ELIZABETH KIMBALL KENDALL was born in America in 1855 and spent much of her childhood in France and Germany. She was greatly influenced by her clergyman father, whose unusually liberal views provided Elizabeth with intellectual stimulus throughout her youth. Her father became American Consul to Strasbourg in the 1870s and later the family lived in Heidelberg, Munich and Paris. This cosmopolitan lifestyle, coupled with Elizabeth's imaginative and adventurous nature, made a comfortable fireside existence an impossibility for her. From early on she showed an adventurous spirit and spent much of her life satisfying her wanderlust.

Elizabeth joined the faculty of the history department at Wellesley College in Massachusetts in 1879, teaching French for a year and then German for four. In 1887 she received a certificate in history at Oxford University, as they did not at that time grant degrees to women, and later received a masters degree from Radcliffe and a doctorate from Boston University. She remained at Wellesley from 1888 until her retirement in 1920, serving as chairwoman of the history department from 1902 until 1920.

Kendall also authored the Source Book of English and two

other books in collaboration with Katherine Comar, then a professor of economics at Wellesley, History of English and A Short History of English. She was also a fellow of the Royal Geographic Society.

Her courses in English, and Far- and Near-Eastern history, were celebrated in part because of the firsthand knowledge she had gained in her many adventures as well as her enthusiasm for her subject. While at Wellesley, Elizabeth's pedagogical approach was "Freedom in teaching is the key to success in teaching". and her open-minded attitude is evident throughout her travels in China as recorded in the book A Wayfarer in China. Her fearless nature, adaptability, and, above all, her fascination with human interactions made her as popular in foreign lands as she was on campus.

Apart from trips to China, Kendall also travelled widely in India, Iran and Tibet. Having retired from Wellesley, she taught for a time at Yenching University in China and later resided in Peking. Ill health eventually caused her to leave, and she lived in England until the outbreak of World War II, when she moved to America. She returned to Somerset in 1922 and died there in 1952 at the age of 97. Jack, her infamous Irish terrier, well known on the Wellesley campus, accompanied her on many of her trips and now lies buried under the Great Wall near Beijing, where he spent his final days.

A Wayfarer in China is Elizabeth's account of a six-month journey in China's western provinces of Yunnan and Szechuan in 1911, during the last quiet months before the revolution which was to shake the country to its core. She was motivated, she said, by "the joy of hunting impressions of strange peoples and strange lands in the out-of-the-way corners of the world".

Having traveled extensively, Elizabeth never felt free from an inner voice, which she said called her night and day to go forth and explore, and she was especially drawn to China.

"Everywhere there is interest, for everywhere there is human nature, but whoever has once come under the spell of the Orient knows that henceforth there is no choice; footloose, he must always turn eastwards."

Undiscouraged by warnings for her safety, she avoided the standard tourist fare in favor of a route that would allow her acquire authentic impressions of the country and its people, noting, "really to see the East one must shun the half-Europeanized town and the treaty port, must leave behind the comforts of hotel and railway, and be ready to accept the rough and the smooth of unbeaten trails."

She could not wait for "freedom from the bondage of conventional life," and above all looked forward to, "the fascination of living among peoples of primitive simplicity and yet of a civilization so ancient that it makes all that is oldest in the West seem raw and crude and unfinished."

The year 1911 heralded in a time of great change in China, and Elizabeth was eager to see the old China before it changed, although, "not the China of the coast, for there the West had already left its stamp", but rather the still-unspoiled China of the interior.

Elizabeth's reasons for going were to observe and learn. She says she did not want to change China – like a missionary, a "conqueror" or a scientist collecting data or specimens – nor did she want to take anything from China bar her impressions of the country, the people and their culture. As she writes in her preface,

"Half a dozen months count for little toward the real understanding of a strange civilization, but it is something to have seen a great people in its home, to have watched it at work and at play, for you have been forced once again to realize that although "East is East and West is West," the thing that most matters is the nature of the man, and that everywhere human nature is much the same."

Elizabeth's journey began in Hong Kong, where she set about preparing for her expedition. She assembled her entourage – an interpreter from Shanghai who spoke English well, a "product of mission schools and a year in an American Western college", and a cook working his way back home to Chung-king (Chongqing), albeit indirectly.

"[A]lthough he spoke no English, he understood European ways and was quick to comprehend my wishes. And he proved a faithful, hard-working fellow, and a very passable cook." The last member of her troupe and "an important part of [her] outfit" was Jack, her small Irish terrier. They left upon a mailboat, The Sikiang, on March 29, headed for the French colonial port of Haiphong.

From Haiphong, Elizabeth and her band caught a train to Yunnan – a distance of about six hundred miles which took them just over three days. In contrast to many European travelers in China at the time, especially female travelers, Elizabeth was unperturbed by her chaotic surroundings and took everything in her stride.

"Everywhere there were other than human travellers; birds, dogs, goats, and pigs were given room, always on condition of having a ticket. I paid four dollars gold for my dog's ticket from Haiphong to Yunnan-fu (today's Kunming), but having paid, Jack's right in the carriage was as unquestioned as mine, and I found this true in all my railway travel in China."

After stopping briefly in Hanoi, her train trundled on across wide, fertile plains framed by distant mountains, fields of rice and maize and walls of bamboo, and then on through dense, tropical vegetation. While observing the passing scenery, she remarked that it was "a delightful region to pass through, perhaps to live in if one were a duck, but for human beings the steamy heat must be very depressing."

Elizabeth then commented on race relations in the region, with a description of the local mistress of a European resident.

"She was what is euphemistically called a "cook " in Tonking; just another name for an arrangement so often resulting from the lonely life of Europeans among a slack-fibred dependent alien population. It is the same thing that confronts the stray visitor to the isolated tea plantations of the Assam hills, where young English lads are set down by themselves, perhaps a day's journey from the next European. What wonder that they find it difficult to hold fast to the standards and principles of the home that seems so far away, or that if they once ignore their inherited traditions, no matter in how slight a thing, there seems to be no natural stopping-place short of the abyss... And the end of it is all black-and-tan babies in the compound."

Moving on, her entourage spent a night at A-Mi-chou in a semi-Chinese inn. There she rejoiced in having broken away from stifling European norms and was at last starting to experience the "real China", which she found considerably more appealing.

"This was truly China, and the European railway with its Frenchified trains and stations seemed indeed an invasion, a world apart."

Overwhelmed by the natural beauty of the mountain scenery of northern Vietnam and southern Yunnan, she described how they were "now making our way up a narrow rocky valley, the gray limestone cliffs gay with bright blue flowers and pink blossoming shrubs... The scenery was very fine and varied; above, the rocky hills, below, the green valleys."

On arrival in Yunnan Fu, Elizabeth didn't find the city itself particularly attractive, but she did appreciate the surrounding countryside, which offered many "charming excursions [with] bright days and cool breezes."

Her time in Yunnan, then at the forefront of China's opium-producing provinces, gave Elizabeth opportunity to reflect upon the issue of opium:

"Although always on the watch for the poppy, nowhere did I see it cultivated... in the main poppy-growing had really been stamped out...Credit where credit is due. Manchu rule may have been weak and corrupt, but at least in respect of one great popular vice it achieved more than any Western power ever thought of attempting."

She also discussed the history and prospects of Yunnan, the presence of hospitals, school, police, and most prominently, the army, and ultimately hope for the future of China.

"Dread of the foreigner underlies much of the present activity and open-mindedness towards Western ideas. The willingness to adopt our ways does not necessarily mean that the Chinese prefer them to their own, but simply that they realize if they would meet us on equal terms they must meet us with our own weapons."

Her point is illuminated through an anecdote:

"At the military school of Yunnan-fu they have a graphic way of enforcing the lesson to be learned. A short time ago the students gave a public dramatic performance... One of the scenes showed an Englishman kicking his Hindu servant, while another represented an Annamese undergoing a beating at the hands of a Frenchman. The teaching was plain. 'This will be your fate unless you are strong to resist.'"

In the previous fifteen years, the French and the British had scoured the province looking for mineral resources and planned out railway routes without giving a thought to the local people. Elizabeth empathized rather with them, saying, "It is not to be wondered at that the people of Yunnan are alive to the danger of foreign interference, for they see the British on the west and much more the French on the south, peering with greedy eyes and clutching hands over the border."

The heavy French presence in Yunnan was immediately apparent.

"Within the capital city the French seem entrenched. A French post-office, a French hospital, French shops, hotels, missions, and above all the huge consulate, are there like advance posts of a greater invasion."

But Elizabeth looked past the politics and problems of the time, concentrating instead on the people as a whole, and says she was well received by all. "Whatever the feeling towards foreigners in the mass, the individual foreigner seemed to meet with no unfriendliness on the part of the people in Yunnan-fu."

The next stage of her journey was a three-week trip north to Ning-yüan-fu (today's Xichang) in the Chien-ch'ang valley. She engaged a "hong", or guild of coolies answerable to a head coolie representative, and was lucky in that she "found [hers] capable, reliable men, adroit in smoothing away difficulties and very ready to meet my wishes." She then hired a sedan chair borne by four men (with room at her feet for Jack), and another for her translator, who insisted on three bearers, complaining that two men was beneath his dignity. They gathered together stores and bedding, sorted out the paperwork and set off from Yunnan-fu to Ning-yüan, which she thought would be "quite off the track of foreigners."

Elizabeth quickly developed a good relationship with her attendants.

"On the march my escort, quick to notice my interest in the flowers, were active in bringing me huge nosegays gathered along the trail, so that my chair was often turned into a gay flowery bower; and they sometimes showed their love for dogs, or perhaps sought to prove their zeal in my service, by picking up Jack and carrying him for the half-hour, to his great disgust, as his sturdy legs were untiring, and equally so was his desire to investigate every nook and corner."

In early April, her caravan departed for Ning-yüan ("It is always a triumphant moment when one's caravan actually starts") with six weeks of travel until reaching Chengtu (Chengdu), the great western capital of China. They planned to go north, traversing the Chien-ch'ang valley after crossing the Yangtze with a detour west at Fulin on the Ta Tu I, so that despite being unable to enter Tibet, she could "see a little of the Tibetans."

She started out, once again blithely disregarding the concerns and warnings of other Europeans that her journey would be too dangerous for a woman alone – alone except for her entourage, of course.

"I did not fear trouble of any sort in spite of a last letter of warning received at Hong Kong from our Peking Legation, but there was just enough of a touch of adventure to the trip to make the roughnesses of the way endurable. Days would pass before I could again talk with my own kind, but I was not afraid of being lonely."

She felt at ease with her hired companions and resolved to treat them more fairly than many of her contemporaries would have.

"It is only when they have been spoiled by overpayment, or by bullying of a sort they do not understand, that the foreigner finds them exacting and untrustworthy. And the Chinese is an eminently reasonable man. He does not expect reward without work, and he works easily and cheerfully."

The group stopped at various villages for the night along the way, and Elizabeth was the center of attention as many had yet to be visited by a foreigner, no less a foreign woman. She was unbothered by their prying curiosity, feeling neither angry nor threatened. At one village, where the window of her room looked out onto the street and was filled with the faces of a staring, curious crowd, pushing each other to get a better view, she demonstrated her patience and good humor. "There was nothing for me to do but wash, eat, and go to bed in public, like a royal personage of former times". In another town, she noted, "Generally they squatted down in a semi-circle about me, settling themselves deliberately to gaze their fill."

Often their arrival in a town prompted complete pandemonium and Elizabeth provided an account of one such instance:

"Our entrance was noisy and imposing. My coming seemed always expected, for as by magic the narrow streets filled with staring crowds. Through them the soldiers fought a way for my chair, borne at smart pace by the coolies all shouting at the top of their voices. I tried to cultivate the superior impassiveness of the Chinese official, but generally the delighted shrieks of the children at the sight of Jack at my feet, and his gay yelps in response, "upset the apple cart."

Elizabeth approved of her coolies' hygiene. They washed themselves thoroughly each day and dressed in loose-cut, well ventilated clothes. In her mind, "there hung about them nothing of the odour of the great unwashed of the Western world."

She didn't, however, share this opinion of the "foul-smelling" inns and often refused the so-called "best room" in favor of "a loft or a stable-yard that had at least the advantage of plenty of fresh air."

Her journey through Yunnan also gave Elizabeth a chance to remark on the province's cultural and ethnic diversity:

"[The Chinese] have not exterminated the aborigines, nor have they assimilated them to any degree. To-day the tribes constitute more than one half the population, and an ethnological map of Yunnan is a wonderful patchwork, for side by side and yet quite distinct, you find scattered about settlements of Chinese, Shans, Lolos, Miaos, Losus...To add to the confusion there is a division of religions hardly known elsewhere...the Mohammedan rebellion of half a century ago has left terrible memories; then add to that the ill-feeling between the Chinese and the tribesmen, and the general discontent at the prohibition of poppy-growing, and it is plain that Yunnan offers a fine field for long-continued civil disorder with all the possibility of foreign interference."

Returning to the road, marching on foot along the great western trade route, Elizabeth marveled at the lush flora and fauna, and remained sympathetic to the impoverished locals. As they passed groups of ruined and abandoned hovels, she reflected on the reasons for their destruction.

"Sometimes the ruin dated back more than a generation to the terrible days of the Mohammedan rebellion. In other cases the trouble was more recent. The irrigating system had broken down, or water was scant, or more frequently the cutting-off of the opium crop had driven the people from their homes."

She was respectful of the religions and traditions of the locals. When she stopped at Che-pei – a small town at an elevation of about 6,000 feet – she found half of her room taken up by a large table set out for the ancestral family worship, and delayed her bedtime to "give the people a chance to burn a few joss sticks, which they did in a very matter-of-fact fashion, nowise disturbed at my washing-things, which Liu, the cook, had set out among the gods."

Arriving in Wu-ting-chou, Elizabeth's entrance was again "a cross between a triumphal procession and a circus show, people rushing to see the sight, children calling, dogs barking, my men shouting as they pushed their way through the throng, while I sat the observed of all, trying to carry off my embarrassment with a benevolent smile. I am told that the interest of a Chinese crowd usually centres on the foreigners' shoes, but in my case, when the gaze got down to my feet, Jack was mostly there to divert attention."

Crossing the mountains separating the Yangtze and Red River basins, they kept off main roads and saw few villages or travelers. After crossing the Yangtze in a large flat-bottomed ferry, they followed a dry river bed for a few miles and stopped in Chiang-yi, nearly 7,000 feet above sea-level, a steep hike which proved too arduous for little Jack:

"[W]e turned abruptly up the mountain-side, by a zigzag trail so steep that even the interpreter was forced to walk. As I toiled wearily upward, I looked back to find my dog riding comfortably in my chair. Tired and hot, he had barked to be taken up. The coolies thought it a fine joke, and when I whistled him down they at once put him back again, explaining that it was hard work for short legs."

They passed through sparse country and stopped in the village of Ho-k'ou, where Elizabeth whiled away a rainy afternoon writing, entertaining the women of the inn with the contents of her dressing case, and smoking long-stemmed, small-bowled pipes with the locals. From there it was a two day journey to Hui-li-chou, a town of about 4,000 inhabitants in the center of an important mining region, during which Elizabeth delighted in the views. They arrived on April 20 and were rushed to their lodging house. Dense crowds swarmed out of restaurants and side streets as the news spread of the arrival of a "yang-potsz" (foreign woman).

"The interest was not surprising, as I was only the third or fourth European woman to come this way, but it was my first experience alone in a large town, and the pressing, staring crowd was rather dismaying."

Next they traveled into the valley of the Anning Ho and towards the Ta Liang Shan, or "Great Cold Mountains", the 300-mile barrier between east and west. This was the country of the independent Lolos, under the governance of tribal chiefs rather than the Chinese. Elizabeth noted:

"Accepting Chinese rule does not generally mean accepting Chinese customs. They hold to their own language and religion… It is very easy to distinguish conquerors and conquered, for the Lolos are darker as well as taller and better formed than the Chinese" Their women, unlike the Chinese Chinese women, wore feminine petticoats and could "stride bravely along on the feet nature gave them."

Although the journey was no longer as fraught with danger, Elizabeth noticed that everyone was very anxious about her safety, "not, of course, from any personal concern for the foreigner, but because the foreigner's Government has such a way of making things unpleasant if anything happens to him."

From Hui-li-chou they traveled further into the Anning valley, past numerous hamlets, rivers and fields along narrow winding paths, as the heat got stronger by the day. Towards evening, they descended abruptly into the Ning-yuan plain where half concealed among the trees lay the town of Ning-yüan-fu – the largest town in the region with a population of about 50,000.

As they rested before entering the town, an incident occurred, which showed that, despite her liberal view, Elizabeth still maintained a sense of otherness. "I saw galloping towards us two horsemen, Europeans, the first I had seen for nearly three weeks. They turned out to be Mr. Wellwood and Dr. Humphreys, of the American Baptist Mission, who had ridden out to make me welcome…It was most delightful to be again among my own kind."

At Ning-yüan-fu, her contract with the hong (business firm) from Yunnan ended and she bid goodbye to her fellow companions, "...sorry to see the Yunnan men go; they were sturdy, willing fellows, quick to learn my ways." She gathered together a new escort, "on the whole younger and smaller than the Yunnan men, but they too did their work well". Her caravan now swelled to seventeen members and she set off on April 29 through the hot and treeless plain for Li-chou, a small, comfortable town at the head of the valley.

From Li-chou the group traveled through the wild and ever-narrowing valley, where the last battles of the Taiping rebellion had been fought, to an inn at Lu-ku, and then into a perilous gorge the next day.

"The trail wound upwards along the mountain-face, often hewn out of the rock and scarcely more than five feet wide, and at one point it was barred effectually by heavy gates. They opened to us, but not on that day half a century ago when the Taiping leader, Shih Ta-k'ai, failing to force his way through, turned back to meet defeat in the wilds above Mien-ning-hsien."

They spent their night at Teng-hsiang-ying, or "Strong-walled Camp", where Elizabeth observed the local Lolo women.

"In feature and colour they might have passed for Italians, and their dress was more European than Chinese in cut. On their heads they wore the Tarn o' Shanter-like cap of black stuff... Altogether the women that I saw had a rather attractive, feminine look, and their manner, though timid, was not cringing. People who know them best have a good word for the Lolos, but few Europeans have come much in contact with them."

The next day they crossed Hsiao Hsiang Ling, or "Little Elephant Pass," spent the next night in the hamlet of Pao-an-ying ("little more than a camp-village") and crossed the Ta Tu Ho

River (here about 600 feet wide) by ferry and headed on to the trading center of Fulin. They entered with the usual fanfare and the addition of "scores of dogs big, gaunt pariahs that infested every village, [which] greeted us as we passed through the gate with a chorus of barks, sending the word down the line. To his credit be it said, Jack paid little attention to them, tittupping along, head up, tail up, only when they came too close turning on them with a flash of white teeth that sent the cowardly brutes flying and brought cries of delight from the village folk who crowded nearer to inspect the strange dog, so small, so brave, and so friendly."

From there they continued along the great tea road by which most of the brick tea consumed by the Tibetans were carried to the frontier market at Tachien-lu. During all hours of the day they passed lines of exhausted yet cheerful men with their ponies and mules, struggling along under their precious burdens.

They then descended 5,000 feet, following the valley of the Ta Tu river and crossing by bridge into Tibet. Continuing on a narrow trail, they occasionally caught glimpses of Tibetan villages along the way: "...no trees; grey, flat-roofed, fortress-like houses, often reached only by a ladder; with few signs of life to be seen even with a glass, there was a forbidding aspect to these places in marked contrast to the bustle of a Chinese village."

They skirted the lower slopes of the Ta Shueh Shan, or "Great Snow Mountains", the out-posts of the Tibetan plateau "between grey cliff and grey river and grey sky" and ascended the valley of the Tarchendo to Tachienlu. People were crossing the rapids on bamboo rope bridges in sling seats, impervious to the fact that one slip could mean certain death. Elizabeth observed that, "the Chinese have no nerves, you know."

After a fight between a soldier in her escort and an inn-keeper over the payment of cakes, Elizabeth noticed the difference between Western and Eastern conduct and "read the man a lesson at so misbehaving himself when escorting a lady, a truly Western point of view which was probably Greek to him."

Tachienlu, where "China and Tibet meet", impressed Elizabeth with its diversity:

"Groups of fierce-looking fellows, clad in skins and felt, strode boldly along, their dark faces bearing indelible marks of the hard, wild life of the Great Plateau...Among them walked impassively the blue-gowned men of the ruling race, fairer, smaller, feebler, and yet undoubtedly master. It was the triumph of the organizing mind over the brute force of the lower animal."

Tachienlu was in the principality of the King of Chala, and the Tibetan population of some 700 families were directly under his authority. But, Elizabeth observed, the Chinese still maintained control, "there is a power behind the throne, and the town is really governed by the Chinese officials, for it is the key to the country to the west, and the Imperial Government has long been awake to the importance of controlling the great trade and military road to Lhasa."

Although she didn't meet the French missionaries in Tachienlu as arranged, Elizabeth was impressed by the native pastor.

"Fine, serene, pure of countenance, he might have posed for a Buddha or a Chinese St. John. In my limited experience of the Chinese, the men who stand out from their fellows for beauty of expression and attractiveness of manner are two or three Christians of the better class. Naturally fine-featured and of dignified presence, the touch of the Christian faith seems to have transformed the supercilious impassiveness of their class into a serenity full of charm. It is a pity that it is not more often so, but the zeal of the West mars as well as mends, and in imparting Western beliefs and Western learning carelessly and needlessly destroys Eastern ideals of conduct and manner, often more reasonable and more attractive than our own. The complacent cocksureness of the Occidental attitude toward Oriental ways and standards has little to rest on. We have reviled the people of the East in the past for their unwillingness to admit that there was anything we could teach them, and they are amending their ways, but we have shown and show still a stupidity quite equal to theirs in our refusal to learn of them."

The caravan turned east towards Ya-chou and crossed the Ma-An Shan Pass at 10,000 feet. They reached Chang-ho-pa, where "The whole village turned out to greet us, and their interest was not to be wondered at, as few Europeans and perhaps no European woman had ever before come this way."

She felt genuine affection she for the locals, and for her men in particular:

"Every one was heedful of my comfort, poking the fire, bringing a fan to screen my face from the heat, drying my shoes, rubbing Jack. The thoughtfulness and good will of my men during all the journey were unfailing, and I never found that friendliness on my part diminished in any way my authority over them."

From Chang-ho-pa they journeyed to Tien-chuan-chou, where the group was delayed when one of her men suddenly hurled himself to the ground in front of the interpreter, "crying out something in beseeching tones, while the other coolies standing about laughed unsympathetically. The poor man was urging the interpreter to ask that I give him back his soul, of which apparently I had deprived him when I took his picture an hour back. Without his soul he would die, and then what would his mother, a widow, do?"

In due course they arrived at Ya-chou and the end of the Lesser Trail. At this point, Elizabeth reflected again on the subject of religion and missionaries in China and what she saw as Christianity's positive influence:

"...there is no doubt as to the reality of Protestant achievement. In Ya-chou the relations of missionaries and townspeople seemed very cordial and natural. Medical work is being carried on, and a hospital was shortly to be opened. But more valuable, perhaps, than any formal work may be the results from the mere presence in the town of Christian men and women living lives of high purpose and kindly spirit...they are the only Europeans in China who are not there for their own personal interests..."

The group passed the small Ming Shan Mountain, famous throughout China for its tea, and continued to Chengtu (Chengdu), where the locals were less impressed by the presence of foreigners. "The people of the plain [of Chengtu] were as friendly as the mountain folk I had been travelling amongst, but they displayed less of the naive curiosity of the out-of-the-way places. Evidently the foreigner was no novelty, nor the camera either."

She considered Chengtu "one of the most advanced cities of China," citing as evidence its university, large arsenal and, the "pride of the moment", a new arcade of shops. "[T]hese are all truly native undertakings, and that, to my mind, is the best part of Chengtu's progress; it shows what the Chinese can do for themselves, not simply following Western leadership."

It was early June when she started the next stage of her journey, a leisurely three-day trip down the Min River to Chia-ting.

"I was tired enough to enjoy keeping still, and lying at ease under my mat shelter I lazily watched the shores slip past; wooded slopes, graceful pagodas crowning the headlands, long stretches of fields yellow with rape, white, timbered farmhouses peeping out from groves of bamboo and orange and cedar, it was all a beautiful picture of peaceful, orderly life and industry."

When she arrived at the rose-red city of Chia-ting, she said it "lives in my memory as a vision of beauty...Built on a sandstone ledge at the junction of the Ta Tu and Ya and the Min, its crenellated red walls rise almost directly from the water, which, when in flood, dashes high against the foundations...standing on the wall one looks down upon a sea of living green from which rise temple and pagoda, or west across Chia-ting plain, perhaps the loveliest and most fertile spot in the Chinese Eden, and then farther west still to where on the horizon towers Omei Shan, the Holy of Holies of Buddhist China."

She commented on "the wonder of the region", a huge Buddha more than 300 feet high, sitting serenely with his hands on his knees, and feet, or what ought to have been his feet, washed by the rushing water of the Ta Fo Rapids.

She then headed off to Mount Omei (Mount Emei), a holy Buddhist mountain steeped in myth and legend.

"On the north the mountain rises by gentle wooded slopes to a height of nearly ten thousand feet above the plain, while on the south the summit ends in a tremendous precipice almost a mile up and down as though slashed off by the sword of a Titan." The found the mountain covered with monasteries, which housed 2,000 monks and 62 shrines, and was the center from which Buddhist teaching was spread throughout the country.

At the summit, the party arrived in the Chin Tien monastery, where Elizabeth spent three peaceful days:

"It seemed but a step from earth to heaven...Two strides back and you are standing awestruck on the edge of the stupendous precipice. The fascination of the place is overpowering, whether you gaze straight down into the black depths or whether the mists, rolling up like great waves of foam, woo you gently to certain death. No wonder the place is called 'The Rejection of the

Body,' and that men and women longing to free themselves from the weary Wheel of Life, seek the 'Peace of the Great Release' with one wild leap into the abyss below."

Elizabeth was deeply affected by her stay on the mountain, noting, "Here on the high mountain-top among these simple minds, the cares and bothers of the life of the plain seemed to fall off. If I came as a sight-seer I went away in the mood of a pilgrim."

Leaving Omei behind, she secured a "wu-pan" river boat and a crew of seven, (including "a small dog known as the 'tailless one'") for the next stage of her journey, down the river to Chung-king (Chongqing). Along the Yangtze she admired the way her men worked together:

"He (the cook) and the Yunnan coolie and the interpreter and the boat people all chummed together very amicably, and I was impressed again, as so many times before, by the essential democracy of China."

In Chung-king Elizabeth was again struck by the Western influence:

"The large foreign community of Chung-king has many elements, missionary, merchant, and officials of the customs, post-office, and consular services. And lying in the river opposite the city are generally English, French, or German gunboats. The relations between all these seem more cordial and helpful than in some treaty ports...on the Chinese side there seemed readiness to appreciate what the West has to offer; in fact the town has a distinctly go-ahead air."

Elizabeth met a French missionary, Mr. Davidson, who, keen to spread the Christian influence yet aware of the difficulties, had founded a social club, "where men of standing, Christian and non-Christian, European as well as Chinese, might mingle on an equal footing... here in the reading and recreation rooms some of the best business men of the city meet for social intercourse, discussions, and occasionally a lecture on such up-to-date subjects as X-rays, tuberculosis, and, very recently, the American Constitution."

The club is managed (very wisely Elizabeth thought) by a Chinese committee to whom she was introduced. They were "quiet, dignified, interested, with the fine manners of the Chinese gentleman, but without the rather lackadaisical superciliousness of some officials, nor was there anything Western about them; they were not copying Europe, but learning how to be a new, fine sort of Chinese." Elizabeth views the club as "a rational and hopeful method of presenting the best of Christian civilization to a class often repelled by missionary propaganda."

She considered, with surprising foresight, the future of the region:

"The next step is assured; before many years have passed, a railway will connect the western capital with Wan-hsien and Hankow, the deserted gorges will no longer re-echo the cries of the trackers, and the upward trip that now takes six weeks will be a matter of two or three days. It will be a different Szechuan then, with its resources exploited, with mines and factories, good roads and fine hotels, a power in the world's market, the goal of the tourist, and I am glad I saw Szechuan before the railway came."

At the eastern end of the gorges, Elizabeth boarded a train to Peking, and after a long and dusty journey checked into the comfortable Hotel des Wagons Lits, keen for her first glimpse of Peking. She was not disappointed.

"There is unfailing charm and interest in the view over Peking from the top of the wall... the wealth of foliage and blaze of colour are almost bewildering; the graceful outlines of pagoda and temple, the saucy tilt of the roofs, yellow and green, imperial and princely, rising above stretches of soft brown walls, the homes of the people, everything framed in masses of living green; and stretching around it all, like a huge protecting arm, the great grey wall."

Elizabeth then decided to travel on to Mongolia with her cook (the "invaluable Wang") and a group of faithful servants. She set off, ignoring warnings from an English officer just returned, who said "the savage Mongol brutes would tear [Jack] in pieces; but I knew my dog and he did not, so I put that aside."

She crossed the grasslands of the Mongolian plateau for four days before seeing other Europeans, with whom she felt an immediate bond.

"I found myself among the new friends that so speedily become old friends in the corners of the world…All told, we were one Swede, one American, one Chinese, seven Mongols, one Irish-man (Jack), and twelve horses."

Together, they crossed through the windy, sun-baked desert for eight days. Nearing the sacred city of Urga, their surroundings became "all so picturesque, so full of Man and colour, that it was more like a play than real life." Visited by thousands of pilgrims each year, it was the home of the Gigin, Bogda or Living God, who ranked third in importance after the Dalai Lama and the Tashi Lama.

After a few days, Elizabeth left Urga, her team, her tent and camp bed, sad that her journey was drawing to an end, reluctant to return to "the uninteresting comforts of Western hotels and trains."

Having lobbed her revolver into a pond to avoid questions from the Russians, who she had been assured would seize it and fine her, she crossed, unchallenged, into Russia and the uninspiring border town of Kiakhta.

"Behind me were the wide, open plains of Mongolia and the

starlit nights in tent or tarantass [a kind of cradle on wheels, drawn by horses]. Here was Russia, half Europe, half Asia, and wholly uninteresting."

From there, Elizabeth went by steamboat to Verchneudinsk, and onto the Moscow Express, homeward bound.

The impressions that Elizabeth took from her travels in China are as illuminating and insightful today as they were when the book was originally published. Although she apologizes to readers presuming to describe somewhere place "so huge, so old, so varied, so complicated" as China, having only been there for a few months, Elizabeth notes that all books about China are informed by the authors particular perspective:

"He has preached to [the Chinese], he has healed them, he has traded with them, and he knows them as the doctor or the trader knows his community. The men and women of the West who have spent their lives in the East have usually gone there with definite purpose and compelling duties. They rarely see more than one part of the whole country, their work holds them fast, and they are prone to see it from the point of view of the interest that took them there."

The traveler, she asserts, has no ulterior motive and no preoccupying purpose, thus their impressions of a country and its culture are much more interesting and informative to people who have not yet been there themselves.

Elizabeth didn't find the Chinese as alien as many of the other Westerners of the time:

"My first and my most lasting impression of the Chinese was how very like they are to us. I had been told… nowhere would you find another country and people so strange, so different from anything before imagined…to my great surprise felt myself almost at home." Though many things seemed bizarre to her Western eyes, "underneath this surface difference the Chinese seemed to me more like ourselves…than any other people of the East that I had known."

She thought this may be due to the fact that the Chinese are not slaves to religion:

"The Chinese, to be sure, is one of the most superstitious of men, but there is little more religion in his fears than is implied in the practices of many a Westerner. He never builds a straight entrance into his house, for he believes that evil spirits cannot move in a curved line; and across the world, people who call him names because of this refuse to sit down thirteen at table."

Elizabeth also found similarities between Western and Chinese attitudes toward industry, saying, "in China material interests have full possession of the field, and the strong man of the Chinese nation is not the soldier or the priest, but the merchant."

She also commented on the Government's role in the life of ordinary Chinese:

"No one inspects the Chinese garbage pail except the pig, or sniffs about for defective drains, or insists upon a man's keeping the roadway in front of his house in order, or compels him to have his children vaccinated. The tyranny of the majority may exist in China, but it is not exercised through the Government. The Chinese as he is today has been fashioned and shaped by long-inherited custom, and the dead hand rests heavily upon him, but he is not a government product, nor is he likely to be just yet…And the Chinese is democratic in very much the same way that the American is…An official career is, in theory, and in good measure in practice, open to the man who is fit, no matter what his antecedents; and the poor boy has quite as good a chance to make himself fit for all save the highest posts, as in America…The Government is weak, the individual or group of individuals strong ; the Government does little, so the other side does much..."

On more mundane matters, she also noted that the Chinese "sit on chairs in preference to sitting on their heels... It is a small thing, but it marks the Chinese off from all other Asiatics, and brings him a little nearer the West[.]"

They also dined in a manner which Elizabeth found identifiable and familiar: "[they] make of dinner a social function, longer and more elaborate, and sometimes even more deadly dull than grand dinners at home."

She disputed the widely-held opinion that China was in a state of decay, an aged, exhausted country:

"I think it must be because everything seems finished in China that people talk about her decay. The whole thing impresses you as having been made and completed, after a fashion, a long time ago..Being a very clever and resourceful people that has lived a long time, the Chinese have found out a great many things for themselves, and as there was no other clever and resourceful people at hand to incite them to other and better ways of doing some things, they went on as they were, neither spending their strength nor sharpening their wits in trying experiments. Indeed, experimenting stopped centuries ago; each natural difficulty, every social and economic problem had been met and answered in some sort of way, and so the people lived year after year, doing things just as their fathers had done them. And now they impress one as very experienced, though old-fashioned; but not aged, no, not at all."

On the contrary she argued that, when face to face with the Chinese at home, "one is overwhelmed by an impression of power, actual power, potential power, power of the individual, power of the group, power well used, power misspent. The impression is almost stunning. You seem to be watching a community of ants, persistent, untiring, organized, only the anthill is a town, and the ants are men physically strong, gluttons for work, resourceful, adaptable, cheerful. Then multiply such ant-hills by thousands and you have China. For not merely is the Chinese the best worker in the world, but he also leads in organization. No Chinese stands alone; behind him is the family, the clan, the guild. He does not confront life naked and solitary, he is one of a group ; that gives him confidence, and keeps him under control."

It is this power of organization which is the most prominent of Elizabeth's impressions of China:

"What was it but this same power of organization that made ready a great revolutionary movement, permeating a population of three hundred odd millions, and spreading over an area of a million and a half square miles, and all so well and secretly done that, though suspected, it could not be discovered?"

Establishing a Republic would have been something completely new to the Chinese, but Elizabeth concluded, correctly, that it was still within reach.

"If they will only bring into play now all their undoubted power of organization, of resource, of moderation, they will certainly make a success of their new experiment in government. Given time, and they will do it. Perhaps my view of China's future is rose-coloured. But the thing seen and felt is of tremendous force, and the impression of power that the Chinese made upon me was rather overwhelming. And, anyway, a friendly opinion may be pardoned in one who, during months of solitary travel in China, never met anything but courtesy and consideration from all, whether coolie on the road, villager or innkeeper, official or priest."

7

MARY GAUNT
A BROKEN JOURNEY

MARY GAUNT'S INCLINATION for veering far from the beaten track – both literally and figuratively – was evidenced very early on in her life. As she wrote in Reflections (1932), "There was always in me a desire for independence considered by mothers in my youth very unwomanly and likely to spoil my chance of marrying. I wanted to travel, a most improper desire for a young lady, I was told."

Born and raised in a small town in Victoria, Australia, she quickly abandoned provincial life, moving to Melbourne as soon as she had finished school and becoming, in March 1881, the first woman to ever matriculate at an Australian university. After disastrous first-year exam results, she abandoned her studies in the Humanities, but carried on with writing. (It was her talent with prose that had won her entry to the university in the first place.)

Her early work drew heavily on the travel tales reported back to her by her five globetrotting siblings. She began publishing her work in Australian literary journals, eventually earning enough from this to fund her own trips to India and England. This first taste of exotic travel – which to this point she had only experienced by proxy – proved the start of a lifelong addiction. Nonetheless, in 1894, after publishing her first novel, Dave's Sweetheart, Gaunt married a local widower, Dr. Hubert Lindsay Miller, and it seemed for a time that she had abandoned her travels for a settled domestic life. Yet, she still insisted on continuing to publish under her maiden name and remained financially independent throughout the marriage.

In 1900, after Miller's sudden death, Gaunt collected her meager inheritance (£30 per annum) and headed to London for its vibrant publishing scene.

Her early days in London were not a wild success. She lived in cramped quarters in Kensington, fighting to break into a writing market which she found to be considerably more competitive than the one she had left in Melbourne. A collaboration with John Ridgewell Essex on a series of adventure stories set in West Africa finally provided her big break. Impressed with her work, her publisher commissioned her to supplement her fiction with writing about her own travels to the Gold Coast and the forts of West Africa (1908-1910). Poorly equipped, traveling with trunks full of flimsy flower and lace-adorned outfits, clumsy photographic equipment and heavy tinned food, she was the only white woman on what proved to be a dangerous journey.

Her first-hand account of these travels, Alone in West Africa, written in chatty prose and with a dry sense of humor, became popular and solidified her career as a travel writer.

Upon the invitation of her cousin, London Times correspondent George Morrison, she traveled to Peking in 1913. Not content to settle into the comfortable routines of expatriate life in the capital, she set out on a mule-drawn cart to the imperial summer resort at Jehol. Upon her return to Peking, she rented a temple in the hills outside the city and began writing her first China narrative, A Woman in China. These adventures failed to satiate her hunger for exploration, and in 1914 she decided to undertake a cross-country trip along the Silk Road, intending to return to Britain along this route by way of Russia and continental Europe. Her journey was interrupted along the way, taking her far from her intended trajectory, but she finally made it back to Europe via a mix of Asian and Russian routes.

The book A Broken Journey was the result of this journey. Gaunt describes her motivations for this second China trip in the introduction:

"Wherein lies the call of the Unknown? To have done something that no one else has done – or only accomplished with difficulty? Where lies the charm? I cannot put it into words – only it is there, the 'something calling – beyond the mountains'…and that voice I heard loudly in China. 'Come and find me! Come and find me!'"

Gaunt continued traveling and publishing travel narratives, novels and short stories well into her sixties, taking trips to the Caribbean and continental Europe. Her hearty short-and-stout physique, coupled with a similarly stalwart character, helped her to carry on well beyond the point where most "well-mannered ladies" of the time would turn back. A vocal feminist, she made a point in her writing of underlining that women could undertake such voyages. It wasn't until the early 1920s that she finally decided to retire to the small village of Bordighera in Italy. Even this period of rest was interrupted, however, this time by World War II and in 1940 she was forced to abandon all of her belongings and flee to the south of France. She died in Cannes in 1942.

The popularity of Gaunt's work can be measured by the fact that it more than supported her wanderlust. Yet due to her relaxed and often self-deprecating style, which generally relayed only her own impressions and experiences rather than scholarly research on the places she visited, she never managed to fully gain admittance to – or recognition from – the elite institutions that 'made' the travel writing stars of her day, like the Royal Geographical Society. As one reviewer of Broken Journey wrote in the Geographical Journal in 1919, "It would be misleading to count it as a serious book of travel, and those who look to it for a matter of general and informative nature will be mislead," before going on to correct many of the errors of geography and spelling that indeed did pepper her work.

The views on China that Gaunt expounds in her writing differ in many ways from the colonialist 'party line'. A radical feminist and atheist, Gaunt's was quite liberal for the time, and she often managed to keep more of an open mind on sensitive issues than many of her (generally male) contemporaries did, finding beauty in China's culture and history where others saw only ignorance or ruins. Yet she never shied away from condemning practices which she viewed as contrary to her own position (for instance, she took a very dim view of the treatment of women in China) and at times she issued blanket condemnations of Chinese society based on single points of contradiction. Twisted through this radical posturing are strands of incongruous Victorian politics and prudishness. At times accepting and sympathetic, and at other times extremely close-minded, her views on China are symptomatic of a society that was (especially for women) in transition.

From the first lines of A Broken Journey, Gaunt's complicated relationship with China is highlighted:

"Everything that I particularly dislike in life, I have met travelling in China; everything that repells [sic] me; and yet, having unwisely invested $10 in an atlas of China, the voice [saying 'Come and find me!'] began to ring in my ears day and night."

The siren's call clearly triumphed over her reservations and she selected an ambitious route. Eschewing cushy train journeys between the Europeanized enclaves favored by her expatriate peers, she decided to embark on a trip westward from Peking, following the Silk Road. She clearly found this road-less-traveled (at least by Westerners) alluring:

"There grew up in me a desire to cross Asia, not by train as I had already done, as thousands of people do every year, but by the caravan route, across Shensi and Kansu and Sinkiang to Andijan in Asiatic Russia, the terminus of the Caspian Railway. Thousands and thousands of people go slowly along that way too, but the majority do not go all the way, and they do not belong to the class or nation whose comings and goings are recorded."

Her enthusiasm for the trip was not widely supported in the comfortable American Presbyterian Mission compound at Pao Ting Fu (today's Baoding), which she made her pre-journey headquarters. As one female missionary put it, "If I wanted to die, I would choose some easier way." Another gentleman advisor, a seasoned diplomat from the Peking Legation Quarter, advised her not to go because of the dangerous and "untrustworthy" Tibetan tribes in Western regions of the country. She was further warned of dying from indigestion, toxic water, rabies and murderous bandits. Even one of her few supporters, a veteran of Mongolian travel, still qualified his remarks with: "The Chinese are fiendishly cruel. Keep your last cartridge for yourself."

Nonetheless, Gaunt found "these remarks made no impression upon me whatever," and she set about preparing for her journey, beginning by assembling her entourage.

She first engaged her "Master of Transport," Tsai Chih Fu.

"He was a fine looking man, dignified and courteous, and I had and have the greatest respect for him…He was a responsible person, a man who would count in any company."

For her interpreter, her choice was much more limited and

her impressions much less charitable.

"Wang Hsien was little and slight, with long artistic hands...
and he was a fool in any language... Could I have chosen, which
I could not, he would have been about the very last man I should
have taken on a strenuous journey as a guide, philosopher and
friend."

Nonetheless, the final member of the little troupe gained her
full approval, a small black and white Pekingese named James
Buchanan who "loved me as no one in the world has ever loved
me."

And then, just as she finished gathering her mismatched
team and stuffing her packs, she received a telegram from Hsi
An Fu (today spelt Xi'an) notifying her that an infamous robber
by the name of White Wolf was on the prowl in Shansi, and
travel for foreigners – let alone single white females – was not
advised. She remained in the compound for several more days,
generously regaled by the missionary team with stories of the
means by which Chinese robbers disposed of Western travelers
and reminiscences of the horrors of the Boxer Rebellion.

Gaunt remained undeterred, relenting only to the extent that
she modified her route, deciding to travel by way of Tai Yuan
Fu (Taiyuan) rather than Xi'an. And thus she set off with puppy,
effeminate translator and steadfast servant in tow.

Leaving Peking for Taiyuan, Gaunt found herself in a first-
class carriage on the self-same railway she had tried to avoid.
The first stretch was short, as the train made a compulsory
overnight stop a few hours from where she boarded. Hosted by
two executives of the British American Tobacco Company, who
lived near the station, she was again plucked from the streets of
the China she had sought to explore and cocooned in foreign-
built luxury. Nonetheless, her evening proved more exciting
than anticipated. A few hours after her arrival, another foreign

woman knocked at the executives' home, cradling her newborn, half-Chinese child and begging for financial assistance so that she could travel to Peking. Gaunt's response to this visitor reveals the depths of the Victorian prejudices lurking within her seemingly liberal views: "And so she was established among us, this woman, who had committed the unpardonable sin of the East, the sin against her race, the sin for which there is no atoning. It is extraordinary after all these years, after all that has been said and written, that Englishwomen, women of good class and standing, will so outrage all laws of decency and good taste…And everyone in the room, while we pitied her, held, and held strongly, that the attitude of the community, foreign and Chinese, was one to be upheld."

Leaving the woman to her fate, Gaunt boarded her train to Tai Yuan the next day, James Buchanan perched squarely on her lap. She admired the countryside, noting the impressive farming terraces eked out of barely arable land. Her evident sympathies with the impoverished locals belied her harsh feelings of the previous evening. She especially lamented the plight of women in the region, noting that few were seen in the fields, most likely because they were crippled by their bound feet. She and Buchanan were jolted out of this peaceful day as they disembarked into the pandemonium of the Tai Yuan train station and met their Tai Yuan hostess, an English Baptist missionary. Immediately the missionary noted that the ever-admirable Tsai Chih Fu still sported a now-out-of-date queue (the required hairstyle of the recently defunct Manchu dynasty, where the front of the head was shaved and the back braided into a long ponytail). She warned that pro-Revolution patrols in the city were known to attack and shear those still coiffed in the imperial style. With impressive sang-froid, Tsai Chi Fu tucked his queue under his cap and announced to the gathered company, "I have always worn one and I like it," and he passed through the town unchallenged.

But Tai Yuan was not a city to which Gaunt warmed. She felt uncomfortable walking the streets alone and was distressed by a palpable anti-foreign attitude. Yet she also noted with some excitement that she felt Tai Yuan to be her true "jumping off place...Here I left altogether the civilisation of the West and tasted the age-old civilisation of the East, the civilisation that was in full swing when my ancestors were naked savages hunting... in the swamps and marshes of Northern Europe."

Jump off she did, leaving Tai Yuan on the back of a feisty pack mule. This did not prove to be an effective mode of transport, as Gaunt found within minutes that she was so uncomfortable that she could not drink in the scenery and "local colour". Finally the discomfort became so extreme that she gave up all together:

"Stay on that pack I could not, so I made my master of transport lift me down, and I sat on the bank for the edification of all the small boys in the district."

She returned to a missionary station and begged for assistance, which she received in the form of a litter. She thus trundled along through Shansi province in what was essentially a tent dangling from poles attached to two unguided mules. This arrangement proved quite fortunate for little James Buchanan, who had nearly died after an altercation with another dog left him crippled. Buchanan's near-death certainly darkened Gaunt's impression of the Chinese, and whenever she got out to take photographs she interpreted his yelps to mean "Don't leave me, don't leave me to the mercy of the Chinese".

Her next stop was the town of Ki Hsien ("very, very crowded, there were hundreds of tiny courtyards and flat roofs"), where she roomed again with a missionary family. During her stay, more news of White Wolf's exploits arrived. While the family poured over the missive, trying to discern whether their friends and colleagues in Xi'an had suffered, Gaunt seemed most occupied with the consequences this would have for her journey.

"I began to fear lest this robber might affect me after all, lest in coming north I was not going to outflank him."

Disregarding the stern warnings of the missionary couple, she resolved to carry on, at least to the large American mission at Fen Chou Fu. On her way, the encroaching threat of which thus far she had been so dismissive was driven home to her: her party passed an impromptu funeral party for a beheaded farmer, almost certainly the work White Wolf's gang.

She arrived at a rundown mission in Ping Yow (Pingyao), where she met a harried young Australian woman waiting anxiously with her five young children for her husband to return from the robber-infested hills. Gaunt spent an afternoon with her reminiscing about the green hills of Victoria and panicking about the Shansi security situation. But the husband returned safely, and nonchalantly pointed out that if he had turned back at every dead body he had encountered along the roads in China, he never would have accomplished his mission. This encouraged her, and so back on the road she went.

While she devoted pages to commentary detailing the pitfalls of missionary work in China and the benefits of her own abstention from religious life, Gaunt stayed in another missionary compound in Shansi, this time in Fen Chou. The industrious ways of this particular missionary crew – more intent on pragmatically improving lives than spreading the "good word" – earned her grudging respect, as did Fen Chou itself. She found it friendly and peaceful, a pleasant contrast to the chaos and danger that had previously dogged her every step. She waxed poetic about its history and architecture, especially two bronze phoenixes guarding the ancient town. While she lamented the decay of important historic features such as the city walls, she remained enthusiastic, daily climbing up the steep ramps to the top of the walls in order to take James Buchanan for a walk and to enjoy the impressive views.

"There were things to be seen from the top of the wall – long lines of camels bearing merchandise to and from the town, donkeys, mules, carts... small footed women seated in their doorways looking out upon the life of the streets, riding on donkeys or peeping out of the tilts of the carts. I could see into the courtyards of the well-to-do, with their little ponds and bridges and gardens. All the life of the city lay beneath us."

Her stay in Fen Chou was extended so that she could better enjoy all that it had to offer: she checked out a temple fair, attended a wedding (where she had her first taste of baijiu, the Chinese alcohol) and visited what she was told was the second-tallest pagoda in China. She appreciated the town's defense system of heaping stones on the top of the wall for hurling at invaders, and she marveled at the scale of the town gates.

"To stand there and look at those great gates, those solid walls, made me feel as if I had somehow wandered into the fourth dimension, so out of my world they were."

Even small details – such as the moon-shaped entrance to the American missionary compound – impressed her with their attention to aesthetic value. It seems Fen Chou – or at least those at the mission station where she stayed – was equally impressed with her, and Gaunt was flattered by the title of respect – "Lao Tai Tai" – which greeted her throughout the compound.

Perhaps as a counterpoint to her glowing reports from Fen Chou, Gaunt suddenly switched track in her narrative, embarking on an extended aside – in a chapter entitled "Miserere Domine!" – on the plight of women in Chinese society at the time of her travels. Proudly flashing her credentials as a suffragette ("a woman is most valuable neither as an angel or a slave, but as a useful citizen"), she bemoaned first and foremost foot-binding and its terrible consequences on the health and welfare of women. She did not let the blame for the situation of women rest solely on Chinese shoulders, but also criticized those Western missions that did not prioritize basic education for women above proselytization, allowing them to remain "toys and pets". She then went on to critique – amongst other things – polygamy, the selling of wives and women's inferior position in relation to men. She concluded: "Amongst the Chinese the five happinesses are: old age, a son, riches, official position and a moustache; so slight a thing is a woman that she does not come into this connection."

Picking up the narrative, Gaunt returned to the road with a slow start, as her muleteers immediately refused to take to the road west of Fu Chou to Sui Te Chou. It was, they warned, a dangerous and lonely route, prone to potentially fatal sandstorms – not to mention robbers – with little recourse to assistance. Gaunt blithely ignored their concerns: "To begin with, I couldn't believe in a Chinese sky where you couldn't see the sun...And as for losing ourselves in the sand – well, I couldn't believe it possible. Always in China, wherever I have been, there had been plenty of people of whom to ask the way."

And so, with the entire party, excepting Gaunt herself – and perhaps James Buchanan –pressing onwards with reluctance, they headed further into the west of China. Her spirits remained high, despite the unhappy demeanors of her team. She even found the ash heaps and rubbish piles on the outskirts of Fen Chou fetching:

"[They were] like little mountain ranges, the refuse of centuries, their softly rounded sides now tinged with the green of springtime." In this way she carried on, enthusiastically underlining how this experience was, for her, akin to moving not only forward along the road, but also back in time, back to the China "in the time of Caesars, further back still in the time of the Babylonish kings, in the days before the first dynasty in Egypt."

The party now only had two mountain ranges and a stony plateau to cross before they reached the Yellow River. Gaunt complained continually that her litter was uncomfortable and her mules untrustworthy on the mountain passes, but she also found the journey fascinating, commenting on the clanging bells attached to the animals and the difficulties of passing other caravans on such narrow tracks. While the roads were full of merchants and travelers, Gaunt found the countryside incredibly impoverished – in one instance becoming ashamed at the sight of a starving man preparing to eat a diseased dog.

Though they often had grandiose names ("The Inn of Increasing Righteousness" and "The Inn of Ten Thousand Conveniences"), she found the available guesthouses much less accommodating than those she had encountered further east. Unwilling to share a single kang (a traditional brick bed heated with coals) in a windowless cave with other guests at the inn, as seemed to be the common practice in the region, she took to sleeping (with James Buchanan) in her litter in the stables. The core sense of Victorian propriety which guided her choice of sleeping arrangements was again evidenced during her meal times:

"Always at midday the litter was lifted off the mules' backs, my table and chair were produced from some recess among the packs, my blue cotton table cloth was spread and Tsai Chih Fu armed himself with a frying pan in which to warm the rice and offered it to me along with hard boiled eggs of dubious age."

Throughout her travels, though she retained the utmost respect for him, Gaunt was continually disappointed with the culinary skills of her master of transport, and she found locally cooked options no more impressive. Nonetheless, she added: "Chinese are connoisseurs in their cooking, but not in poor villages in the mountains in Western Shansi, where they are content if they can fill their starving stomachs. To judge Chinese taste by the provisions of these mountaineers is as if we condemned the food of London, having sampled only those shops where a steak pudding can be had for fourpence."

In this impoverished region, Gaunt acutely felt the cultural and linguistic divide between herself and those around her. In most towns, she quickly became the center of attention, as foreigners – especially women – were scarce in such lonely and barren territory.

"Men and women stared at the foreign woman with all their eyes, for foreigners are rather like snow in June in these parts, and my coming made me feel as if a menagerie had arrived in the village, so great and interested were the crowds that assembled to look at and comment on me."

Even with the aid of a translator, she still felt apart, noting that this feeling was exacerbated by the disconnect between the information that Wang Hsien gathered and that which he passed on to her. She also noted that he frequently did not ask the questions that she requested he ask of others; finding her queries impolite, he made up his own answers in order to save her face.

The treacherous trek over the first set of mountains brought the party eventually to the city of Yung Ning Chou, where Gaunt was keen to make the acquaintance of a band of Scandinavian missionaries who – in twenty years of service in the region – had not yet made any converts. Unfortunately, the unsuccessful Scandinavians were out of town, but she did manage to track down a Norwegian woman heading for a convent in the nearby hills. Gaunt found her to be "a pathetic figure of sacrifice, a wistful woman who was giving of her very best and yet was haunted by the fear that what she was giving was of very little worth, surely the most bitter and sorrowful reflection in this world." She seemed almost gleeful at the failure of these "pathetic" missionaries, as if their plight reinforced her own atheism.

Departing from the lonely Norwegian, the party carried on to the nearby village of Liu Lin Chen, where news of the exploits of White Wolf again threatened the trip. Gaunt's midday meal was interrupted when Wang Hsien and the muleteers raced over in a frenzy and announced – with no shortage of dramatic antics – that the gates of Sui Te Chou (the next major city on her itinerary) had been closed for four days for fear of an invasion by White Wolf. This was a major blow.

"If I would go to Lan Chou Fu and on through Sin Kiang to the Russian border, through Sui Te Chou I must go. There was no other way. These days in the mountains had shown me that to stray from the caravan road was an utter impossibility."

While Gaunt realized that her journey could not now be completed, she made a shock announcement to the team (who was convinced they would be turning back imminently): "We will go on to the Yellow River." With that, as if on cue from a heavenly stage manager, a gentle rain began to fall.

Pushing onward, the party headed for the next town, Hsieh Ts'un. Gaunt tried to describe it diplomatically:

"'It is better,' says a Chinese proverb, 'to hear about a thing than to see it,' and truly on this journey I was much inclined to agree with that dictum."

The village was dirty and impoverished, even more so than those she had encountered elsewhere in the mountains of Shansi. It rained almost continually during her stay, halting her progress and leaving her chilly and damp (with only her trusty Burberry rain jacket to protect her). The only bright spot during her time in the town seemed to be her interactions with the locals. As usual upon her arrival, she immediately became a person of interest, and all of the villagers turned out to have a look at her. When she decided to retire and requested some privacy, she was impressed by their willingness to cooperate.

"All honour I give to those poor peasants of Western Shansi, I was undisturbed. I am afraid a lonely Chinese lady would hardly be received with such courtesy in an English village were the case reversed."

Nonetheless, as her time in the village dragged on, as the rain continued to fall and as reports on White Wolf's progress became more frequent, erratic and exaggerated, she became disheartened.

"That day I was distinctly unhappy and more than a little afraid. I was alone among an alien people who only regarded me as a cheap show; I had no one to take counsel with, my interpreter only irritated me, and to add to my misery I was very cold. I have seldom put in a longer or more dreary day than I did at Hsieh Ts'un."

Finally, the weather cleared and the party set off on the final leg of the journey to the Yellow River. The road was steep, and for one of the first times on her journey, Gaunt insisted on walking. Her asthma slowed her considerably, but she persisted, and, as she reached the summit of the first peak, she found her efforts rewarded:

"And then I knew it was worth it all – the long trek from Fen Chou Fu, the dreary day at Hsieh Ts'un, the still more dreary nights, this steep climb which took more breath than I had to spare – for the view when I arrived at the point of vantage was beautiful…Beautiful, beautiful, with entrancing loveliness is that view over the country up in the hills that hem in the Yellow River as it passes between Shansi and Shensi."

Her mood turned somber, though, as she contemplated

the fate of the poverty-stricken peasants who inhabited these beautiful hills. She noted with sorrow that the mineral riches recently discovered in the region would most likely not improve their situation:

"Unexploited, the people are poor to the verge of starvation; worked, the delicate loveliness of the country-side will vanish as the beauty of the Black Country has vanished, and can we be sure that the peasant will benefit?"

From this mountain vantage point, the team carried on over the mountain range and Gaunt caught her first glimpse of the river which she had struggled for weeks to reach:

"And at last through a cleft in the hills, I saw one of the world's great rivers and – was disappointed."

They eventually reached the anti-climatic river crossing itself, a grimy temple town called Chun Pu, where bedraggled soldiers haphazardly rifled through her luggage. Despite feeling deflated, Gaunt celebrated her arrival at the end point of her now-curtailed journey by distributing raisins among the children and allowing the locals to look through the view-finder of her camera – on the condition that ladies preceded men in the queue, much to their confusion.

"Then I had one more good look at the river, my farthest point west on the journey, the river I had come so far to see. It was so peaceful in the afternoon sunlight that it seemed foolish not to go on. The hills of Shensi beckoned and all my fears fell from me… Then reason came to me… and I turned sadly and regretfully and made my way back to Fen Chou Fu."

With the benefit of hindsight, the later conceded that had she carried on, she would have arrived in Russia at the outbreak of World War I, making her change of plans a blessing in disguise.

"Perhaps when the world is at peace I shall essay that fascinating journey again. Only I shall look for some companion, and even if I take the matchless master of transport I shall most certainly see to it that I have a good cook."

Almost from the moment she turned back, Gaunt was tormented by the notion that she was in dishonorable retreat.

"Well, I had failed! The horrid word kept ringing in my ears."

She became paranoid about the responses of those she met on her way back, interpreting them to mean that she had "given in too easily" or "turned back at a shadow." She even began to question whether, given a better cook, she would have carried on, and this left her feeling even more humiliated. A chance meeting with Reginald Farrer – who had also been traveling in the region on a botany research trip – somewhat allayed her fears, as he conceded he was certain she had been disposed of by White Wolf weeks before. She began to discuss her recent adventures with the very pro-China Farrer, and here the impact of her feminist leanings on her impressions of China were clarified:

"We discussed our travels, and we took diametrically opposite views of China. But it is impossible to have everything: one has to choose, and I prefer the crudeness of the new world, the rush and the scramble and the progress, to the calm of the Oriental. Very likely this is because I am a woman. In the East, the woman holds a subservient position, she has no individuality of her own, and I, coming from the newest new world, where woman has a very high place indeed, is counted a citizen, and a useful citizen, could hardly be expected to admire a state of society where her whole life is a torture and her position is regulated by her value to the man to whom she belongs."

With this in mind, Gaunt continued on her trip back her starting point. She decided to skip the missions this time, preferring Chinese country inns. During this quiet trip through the countryside, she reflected further on the peasants she saw working in the fields, elaborating her views on the country.

"Wherever I went in China, it was impressed upon me, that man was the least important factor in any work of production. He might be used till he failed and then thrown away lightly without a qualm. There were plenty glad enough to take his place."

This lack of individuality depressed her. Yet small bright spots broke through her somber mood. On one of her last days on the road, after a particularly rough night in a flea and rat-infested inn, her interpreter led her to a small temple. Expecting little, she was dazzled by the beauty of the spot and again felt able to appreciate Chinese culture:

"What has a nation that could produce such a temple to learn from the West? I shall never forget the carved dragons in red and gold that climbed the pillars at the principal entrance, the twisted trees, the shrines over the springs and the bronze figures that stood guard on the platform at the entrance gate... The whole place was typical of the decay that China allows to fall upon her holy places; but seen in the glamour of the early morning, with the grass springing underfoot, the trees in full leaf, the sunshine lighting the yellow roofs and the tender green of the trees, it was gorgeous."

Soon after visiting the temple, the party arrived back at the railway line running through Tai Yuan Fu, and Gaunt jumped at the opportunity to dispense with her unsatisfactory interpreter.

"At Tai Yuan Fu, I paid Mr. Wang's fare back to Pao Ting Fu and bade him a glad farewell. There may be worse interpreters in China, but I really hope there are not many... I believe he did get back safely, but I must confess to feeling on sending him away as much as I should do were I to turn loose a baby of four to find his way across London."

After a short sojourn in Tai Yuan Fu, she finally returned by train to her starting point, Pao Ting Fu.

"There are days we always remember all our lives – our wedding day and such-like – and that coming back on the warm summer's day out of the hot, dusty streets of the Western suburb into the cool, clean, tree-shaded compound of the American missionaries at Pao Ting Fu is one of them."

And yet, this was not the end of the line for Gaunt and her faithful pup. After a short period of recuperation and some entertaining evenings spent with old friends, she prepared her cases to follow a revised itinerary: by boat eastward to the treaty port of Tientsin, then northward by rail through the Japanese and Russian-controlled territory of Manchuria to Kharbin, by steamer along the Amur River, which divides Russia and China, and definitively out of China and across Russia (with the intention of traveling through Siberia and continental Europe).

After stocking up on merchandise allegedly looted during the Revolution, Gaunt boarded a small boat and enjoyed several days of leisurely sailing towards Tientsin. Arriving in the city, she checked into the Astor House hotel, and immediately found herself in a world quite divorced from the China with which she had become so well acquainted.

"Tientsin was a place apart, not exactly Chinese as I know China – certainly not Europe; it remains in my mind as a place where Chinese art learns to accommodate itself to European needs. All the nations of the world East and West meet there."

She noted that the city "wasn't any good to her" because it had already been so thoroughly discussed in other travelogues – and also found the climate uncomfortably hot. It was therefore with little regret that she and James Buchanan boarded a train to Kharbin via Mukden. She met a very international crowd on the train – a British Marine studying Chinese and a Japanese Naval Officer studying French – and found the amenities on board quite satisfactory, a relief after her experiences in Shansi. Her only major issue was that, while riding on a Japanese controlled train from Mukden to Chang Ch'un, poor James Buchanan was forced to travel in a cage in the animal carriage. By contrast, on their next (Russia-managed) train, Gaunt discovered she had no money left to cover Buchanan's fare. A Russian ticket officer gallantly resolved the issue by covering the dog with a cushion and pretending it didn't exist.

"[Buchanan] told me how infinitely preferable from a dog's point of view are the free and easy trains of Russia and China to the well-managed ones of Japan."

While still in China, Gaunt noted the countryside was becoming increasingly Russianised, with Russian modes of dress more common, roubles in circulation and dairy products available in the markets. Arriving in Kharbin, this was especially apparent:

"In fact to all intents and purposes [Kharbin] is Russian. There were Russian students all in uniform in the streets, and bearded, belted drivers drove the droshkies with their extra horse in a trace beside the shafts, just as they did in Russia."

Upon arriving in the city, she impulsively accepted the invitation of a forthright porter named "Mr. Poland", a Polish Jew, to stay at his home rather than at the city's main hotel. She spent a pleasant few days being cared for by the "Poland" family, who generously helped her prepare for her journey along the Amur River. Her impressions of the city were quite positive – though the weather remained uncomfortably hot, she enjoyed the scenery.

"The gardens at Kharbin are a great institution. There in the summer's evening, the paths were all lined with lamps; there were open air restaurants; there were bands and fluttering flags; there were the most excellent ices and insidious drinks of all descriptions, and there were crowds of gaily dressed people –

Monte Carlo in the heart of Central Asia!"

After bidding a fond farewell to the Poland family, Gaunt boarded a train to Vladivostock and then on to Khabarovsk, where she caught a steamer traveling along the Amur River. As she progressed further away from China, she noted "there were Chinese still on the stations, but they were becoming more and more Russianised. They still wore queues, but they had belted Russian blouses and top-boots, and they mixed on friendly terms with flaxen-haired, blue-eyed Russians similarly attired."

From the ship's deck, she rejoiced at the sight of the green, flower-covered fields and dense forests on the Russian side of the river that were so lacking in China. She soon began to lament the wanton destruction of these forests, as she realized that large swathes of trees had been felled to power the steamers such as hers.

As World War broke out in Europe, Gaunt traveled with many difficulties westwards across Russia and eventually made it to safety in Sweden, with Buchanan still by her side.

8

Roy Andrews
Camps and Trails in China

WITH HIS OFT-STATED preference for blasting off rifles rather than peering patiently through field glasses, Roy Chapman Andrews was the prototypical all-American outdoorsman of the early twentieth century. Working in the name of science, or more precisely, that of the American Museum of Natural History in New York, he undertook a career's worth of expeditions across Asia, where, as a combination of big game hunter and Indiana Jones-esque adventurer, he pillaged the wilderness and cultural centers of the Orient in order to fill out the museum's collections.

His route to becoming one of his country's top naturalists follows the classic American Dream narrative. Born into an average middle class Midwestern family, he was enchanted with the natural world from a young age and was also gifted at dispensing with Nature's living treasures at the squeeze of a trigger. After graduating from college, he bought a one-way ticket to New York and begged the American Museum of Natural History for a job. Offered only a janitorial post, Roy's determination allowed him to rise through the ranks. His obituary in Science magazine diplomatically describes his ascent: after producing a series of mediocre scientific monographs, Roy wisely decided to seek other avenues, "and he developed an overwhelming desire to carry on field work and exploration." For almost two decades he traveled extensively across Asia on museum business, beginning with a Japanese whale hunting expedition and culminating in a series of lavish convoys across Mongolia in search of the "origins of man." (Unfortunately such "origins" were never uncovered, but these expeditions are credited with some key paleontological finds, such as the first discovered dinosaur eggs.) His brilliant maneuvers in the field eventually won him the position of president of the museum, a far cry from his earlier positions.

Of his wife and co-author, Yvette Borup Andrews, much less is known. Daughter of a wealthy American family, she studied art and photography at elite academies in Germany during the interwar period (eventually becoming a close personal friend of Kaiser Wilhelm's daughter). Directly after her return to the US, her brother introduced her to Roy and they were soon married. Their wedding announcement in the society pages of the New York Times alludes to the hero-sidekick dynamic that characterized their relationship: "Within a year, Mr. Andrews intends to have his wife accompany him on an exploring expedition." Yvette, it must be noted, preferred to do her shooting with a camera rather than a gun, but was able to help out with the "real" hunting when called upon.

Camps and Trails is the narrative of the newlywed Andrews' first extensive expedition in Asia. Accompanied by a big game expert named Heller (and a convoy of servants, muleteers and 31 pack mules), for over a year, from 1916 to 1917, they scoured China's Yunnan Province for evidence of new animal species. The book provides a revealing glimpse into Roy's early impressions of a continent that became so important to his future. Undertaken during World War I, it is also a snapshot of international opinions in far-flung corners of the globe during a historical turning point.

In 1930, many expeditions later, the gathering clouds of World War II made Roy Andrews' continued research in Asia untenable, and he returned permanently to New York. He divorced Yvette and, after his stint in the museum president's chair, retired to spend the next 20 years penning accounts of his numerous adventures. Perhaps still stung by his early failures in research, his written work is generally of the "popular science" variety, and he pointedly abstains from going into the "details," which he generally leaves to the museum science staff. His writings perpetuate his adventurer persona with tales of near-death experiences, shoot-outs and run-ins with the ever-troublesome natives. A man of his times, Andrews made the most of the opportunities for testosterone-fuelled "science" expeditions that were still possible in those times. The China he describes to his readers had much to offer a gun-toting naturalist. However, he often finds the politics and natives of the country problematic, because they "conspire" to hinder his work. The general picture of China that emerges is one of incredible natural beauty, interrupted ever too frequently by Chinese society.

Before the Andrews' "Asian Zöological Expedition of the American Museum of Natural History" had even begun, tales of the expedition had generated such animated press reports across the US that they found themselves bombarded with letters from citizens of all stripes – from butchers to nursemaids – offering their services and begging to be allowed to join the trip. As they chugged along from New York to San Francisco to catch an Asia-bound steamer, they noted wryly that enthusiastic applicants continued to "besiege" them at every station. With their celebrity status drawing massive crowds, they pushed off to much fanfare. Excitement levels dropped off sharply as the ship headed to sea, and their voyage to China via Japan and Korea was uneventful.

The political turmoil in China at the time guaranteed an end to the hum-drum. President Yuan Shi-kai had recently attempted to reinstate the dynastic system with himself as emperor, sparking violent revolts in the southern provinces to which Andrew and his party were bound – a potentially disastrous situation for their research. His attitude toward these political circumstances in China is revealing of his position toward the country in general: if the circumstances suited the expedition, they were commendable, and if they got in the way, they were "backward" and bad. So, while they criticized Yuan for attempting to destroy China's fledgling democracy (a rejection of the Western values they proudly supported), they went on to note that, as the popular uprisings threatened their journey, they "hoped that Yuan would be strong enough to crush this rebellion as he had that of 1913."

Fortunately for the Andrews, while the rebellions were not brutally suppressed, the political situation was deemed sufficiently stable by Chinese officials for them to obtain the assorted visas and stamps needed to carry on. They spent a pleasant week in Peking collecting the documents while enjoying the cosmopolitan surrounds of the Legation Quarter. The only dark spot on this idyllic stay was that, because of "international complications" (World War I), their "social intercourse was extremely limited." Still, they didn't let that distract them from enjoying themselves, and they even seemed to find the rocky political situation (at least in China) delightfully entertaining. As they described Peking, "talk is all of horses, polo, racing, shooting, dinners, and dances, with the interesting background of Chinese politics, in which things are never dull. There is always a rebellion of some kind to furnish delightful thrills, and one never can tell when a new political bomb will be projected from the mysterious gates of the Forbidden City."

Passports duly stamped, they headed for Shanghai, and, by

the time they arrived, Yuan Shikai had died. The political situation remained chaotic, but the revolts in the south dissipated and the Andrews carried on south to the city of Foochow. Away from the well-appointed foreign quarters of Beijing and Shanghai, their spirits were quickly brought low by the conditions they found. To them, Foochow was "filthy" and "offensive". Inspired by the town's putrid streets and fetid conditions, Roy remarked: "No matter how long one has lived in China one remains in a condition of mental suspense unable to decide which is the filthiest city of the Republic."

Engaging a small crew and travelling with light gear, they headed off from Foochow to meet an American missionary, Reverend Harry Caldwell, in the wilds of Fukien Province, to help him dispose of a blue tiger that was terrorizing his neighborhood. At the way station where they had agreed to meet him, they were warmly greeted by locals with blasts of fireworks and enthusiastically escorted by troops of children to their temporary accommodation in a missionary compound. The Andrews did not reciprocate the locals' enthusiasm. They were angered to find curious faces pressed against their windows at night, and were absolutely livid when the residents of a neighboring courtyard deigned to wake early and go about their daily business while the Andrews were still trying to sleep. "Boiling with rage we dressed and went for a walk, vowing not to spend another night in the place."

With little regret, they packed up and headed with Caldwell to his permanent residence at Yen-Ping, which they found much more to their taste: "Yen-ping is a wonderfully picturesque old city, situated on a hill at a fork of the river...Mr. Caldwell's residence commands a wonderful view down the river and in the late afternoon sunlight when the hills are bathed in pink and lavender and purple a more beautiful spot can hardly be imagined."

Happily ensconced, they finally began to investigate their natural surroundings and tuck into their first hunt. Their immediate findings were not positive. They lamented the widespread deforestation of the area, which had severely reduced the wildlife population. They also found their attempts to hunt hindered by the Chinese, who were either "continually at work in the fields" where the animals were to be found or because, in the case of their employees, they were difficult to organize and control. Nonetheless, when they ventured to set up field camps outside Yen-Ping, they experienced limited success in hunting large game and bagged what seemed to be most of the region's bat population. Yvette described the bat collecting experience, which involved squelching through guano-filled caves and beating the bats to death with bamboo switches:

"It is a rather terrifying experience for a girl to sit in a bat cave especially if the light has gone out and she is in utter darkness. Of course she has a cap tightly pulled over her ears, for what girl, even if she be a naturalist's wife, would venture into a den of evil bats with one wisp of hair exposed! All about is the swish of ghostly wings which brush her face or neck and the air is full of chattering noises like the grinding of hundreds of tiny teeth. Sometimes a soft little body plumps into her lap and if she dares to take her hands from her face long enough to disengage the clinging animal she is liable to receive a vicious bite from teeth as sharp as needles. But, withal, it is good fun, and think how quickly formalin jars or collecting trays can be filled with beautiful specimens!"

The bat massacre was interrupted when an urgent message was received from Yen-Ping, ordering them to rush back from the field to the safety of Caldwell's missionary compound because rebels were approaching the city. The Andrews were genuinely thrilled by this "diverting" adventure. They wanted to savor the experience, and so first sat down to a proper (if rushed) three-course lunch to discuss events.

"The servants began to pack the loads at once and meanwhile we ate a roast chicken faster than good table manners would permit – in fact, we took it in our fingers. We were both delighted at the prospect of some excitement and talked almost as fast as the Chinese."

Their eventual trip back to town was an arduous trek uphill in steaming temperatures. They passed many less fortunate peasants (without armies of luggage-bearing coolies) also fleeing to Yen-Ping. Yvette noted with genuine sympathy that many women could hardly walk on their bound feet and it seemed doubtful that they would make it to safety. As encouragement, she offered them bits of cake and was deeply hurt by their lack of enthusiasm for the gift.

As dusk was falling, they arrived back at Caldwell's compound, entering through a secret backdoor system of ladders to evade detection. The rebels had invaded earlier in the day and government troops were en route to Yen-Ping to recapture the city. Hundreds of refugees pounded on the gates of the missionary compound, but were turned away because it was agreed that sheltering Chinese would endanger the lives of the foreigners, who would lose their consular protection. Still enthusiastically following the developments but perhaps not absorbing the severity of the situation, Roy noted, "A real battle could be expected and it was very likely that the city would be partly destroyed. We had a picnic supper on the Caldwell's porch and discussed the situation."

The next day, before the army had even arrived, a burst of fighting broke out within the city between rival rebel factions. After this died down, the Andrews pinned "crude red crosses" to their shirts and went about collecting the wounded and transporting them to the missionary hospital. As they modestly described their efforts, the Chinese residents "got right there a lesson in Christianity which they will not soon forget."

Fighting started again, this time between the newly-arrived government troops and the rebels. During a momentary ceasefire, the missionaries jumped into action, brokering a peace deal involving a ceasefire in exchange for twenty "traitors". The Andrews declared themselves heroes alongside the missionaries, and the city officials echoed this sentiment:

"The following day twenty brigands were given a so-called trial, marched off to the west gate, beheaded amid great enthusiasm, and the incident was closed. In the afternoon a messenger called and delivered to each of us an official letter from the commander of the Northern troops thanking us for the part we had played in averting trouble and bringing the matter to a peaceful end."

The Andrews and Caldwell then headed back off into the wild to hunt the infamous blue tiger. Caldwell was an expert tiger hunter and entertained the Andrews with many thrilling tales of tigers terrorizing (snacking on) the locals. The hunt proved no less colorful. At one point, they came within inches of getting the blue tiger, but several Chinese woodcutters, shrieking at the prospect of being mauled on their walk home, disturbed it before they could fire. Roy was enraged by the men, lamenting, "it was only by exercising almost superhuman restraint that we prevented ourselves from doing bodily harm to the three Chinese who ruined our hunt."

A few weeks later, the champion hunter Heller joined their party and they moved camp to a Taoist temple in the nearby hills. The team was fascinated by the rituals of the Taoist community, but they took a much darker view of the priests themselves:

"The priests who shuffled about the temples were a hard lot. Most of them were fugitives from justice and certainly looked the part, for a more disreputable, diseased and generally undesirable body of men I have never seen."

At this point, they had been unsuccessfully tiger hunting for five weeks. Frustrated and grouchy, it was with little regret that the museum team decided to call it quits, bid farewell to Mr. Caldwell and his elusive tiger, and head to Hong Kong to restock before starting their travels in Yunnan.

In Hong Kong, they supplied their caravan lavishly, filling almost one hundred trunks. Roy elucidated their philosophy on such matters:

"When an expedition expects to remain in the field for a long time it is absolutely necessary to be as comfortable as possible and to live well; otherwise one cannot work at one's highest efficiency."

They carried everything from tents, cots, and tinned American food to novels and games. They also packed some higher-tech equipment including a portable dark room and a "moving picture" camera. Perhaps their most important acquisition in Hong Kong, however, was a human resource, their interpreter and "head boy" Wu Hung-tao. Despite their generally negative impression of almost every Chinese person they encountered, they had nothing but praise for Wu.

"Wu proved to be the most efficient and trustworthy servant whom we have ever employed, and the success of our work was due in no small degree to his efforts."

Thus supplied, they hit the road for Yunnan via Vietnam. Their first stopover was at a leper hospital at Paik-hoi. Although their host was away when they arrived, they proceeded to make themselves at home in what was apparently quite a cushy leper colony.

"When [our host] returned he found us in his drawing room comfortably enjoying afternoon tea...and watching some remarkably fine tennis."

Making their stay even more pleasant, he helped the team engage an English-speaking cook, who they immediately christened "the Woolworth Building" because of his astonishing height. Finding it incredibly entertaining to give their employees such "screamingly funny" nicknames, they continued the practice throughout the trip.

Their next stop, at Haiphong, was not nearly so enjoyable. They were distressed by the sloppy work of the baggage handlers – one accidentally dropped a box into the river – and they employed "well directed kicks" to get them to shape up.

From here they journeyed to Hanoi ("a city of delightful surprises") and then finally, by rail, to Yunnan. The team were awed by the quality of the French engineering on the railway between Vietnam and Yunnan, which traversed jagged, mountainous terrain and enthusiastically applauded the French for overcoming "obstacles" such as the fact that "while it was being built through the fever-stricken jungles of Tonking the coolies died like flies."

Finally they pulled up in Yunnan-Fu (the capital of Yunnan), ready to roll up their sleeves and get to work, but social engagements with the Yunnan-Fu expatriate community intervened.

"We thought that after leaving Hongkong our evening clothes would not again be used, but they were requisitioned every night for we were guests at dinners given by almost everyone of the foreign community."

Managing to bid their generous hosts farewell, they set their caravan in motion and made for the hills. They found the diminutive ponies of Yunnan much too stumpy for comfort.

Their statuesque cook ("Woolworth Building") was especially miserable, and his unhappiness only increased when it started raining a few hours after setting off, forcing him to squish into ill-fitting oilskins. This made the team "roar with laughter" and Heller promptly renamed him "Yellow Peril", The "wide girthed" Heller later paid for his rude jabs, almost crushing his own tiny pony.

Heller's pony survived and the team spent several quiet weeks trundling through the mountains towards their designated research area. They found their mule drivers to be difficult to control ("Force seems to be the only thing they understand and kindness produces no results") and the road quality terrible ("The Chinese have a proverb which says: 'A road is good for ten years and bad for ten thousand,' and this applies most excellently to those of Yün-nan").

But mostly they had a grand old time, carousing round the campfire at night and taking in the scenery by day. At the town of Chu-hsuing, two remarkable happenings interrupted this peaceful amble into the hills. First, Heller's pony – perhaps overwhelmed by the thought of continuing to shuffle along under her spine-cracking load – threw herself off a bridge while his back was turned, survived the fall and tried to escape into a meadow. Her prison break was unsuccessful and she was soon back at work. Second, they encountered Ms. Cordelia Morgan, a young missionary and niece of a prominent American senator, who was living alone in the town. They were dazzled by her bravery, the only white person in such a remote area "surviving solely on Chinese food." They generously treated her to a dinner of their tinned delights before continuing onward the next day.

Finally, over a month after setting off, they arrived in Li-Chiang, where they intended to set up their first specimen gathering camp. They were greeted by stares from the startled populace. As Yvette put it, "I felt as though I were the chief actor in a circus parade at home".

However, the shock turned to delight when the research team announced they would pay cash for any animal specimens. For the next several weeks, their camp – set up in a temple outside of town – was packed with a stream of townsfolk bearing frogs, snakes and small mammals. The team also had collected so many animals from their own traps and hunting expeditions that, by the time they were ready to leave Li-Chiang, the mammalian, reptilian and amphibian populations of the area had been satisfactorily decimated. The only real problem encountered during their stay was that the locals began stealing the museum team's sophisticated traps, using them to catch samples to be sold to the expedition.

With their collections thus enriched, they decamped and headed for the true wilderness of Yunnan, the Snow Mountain range. Several days of drizzle and mist left them soggy and irritable, but once the clouds cleared, they were astounded by the stunning natural beauty of the area:

"On the morning of October 11 we awoke to find ourselves in another world. We were in a vast amphitheater of encircling mountains, white almost to their bases, rising ridge on ridge, like the foamy billows of a mighty ocean. At the north, silhouetted against the vivid blue of a cloudless sky, towered the great Snow Mountain, its jagged peaks crowned with gold where the morning sun had kissed their summits...It was an inspiration, that beautiful mountain, lying so white and still in its cradle of dark green trees. Each hour it seemed more wonderful, more dominating in its grandeur, and we were glad to be of the chosen few to look upon its sacred beauty."

Despite their remote location, they were visited a few days later by an Austrian botanist, Baron Haendel-Mazzetti, who had arrived in Yunnan several years earlier to study the flora of the area. At the outbreak of World War I, the Baron had become stranded, unable to exit Yunnan through any of the usual routes – Tibet, Burma or Tonking (Vietnam). By the time he crossed paths with the Andrews, he had been trapped in the province for over two years, was out of money and the only remaining option was to make the four-month overland journey to Shanghai. They noted unsympathetically that "his enjoyment of our coffee, bread, kippered herring, and other canned goods was almost pathetic," but conversation (so long as they avoided awkward "war talk") was interesting and he had many useful research tips for the area. (Shortly after meeting them, the unfortunate Baron did indeed head for Shanghai, but by the time he arrived, China had joined the war and it was also a closed to him. Whether he ever made it back to Austria remained a mystery for the team.)

To assist with big game hunting around Snow Mountain, the team hired several native Moso hunters. Although the men were "poorly equipped" with crossbows, they soon proved to be expert at catching the local game and at times were even more successful than the museum squad armed with modern rifles. They were especially impressed with the work of one hunter, Hotenfa, who remained for the entire trip to northern Yunnan, even after the other Mosos left. A special favorite of the Andrews, though never considered their equal, "He was one of the most intelligent, faithful, and altogether charming natives whom we met in all Yün-nan. He was an uncouth savage when he first came to us, but in a very short time he had learned our camp ways and was as good a servant as any we had."

These hunts on Snow Mountain were spectacularly successful. On the first day, Roy managed to blast a full-grown goral right off the mountain. The entire party gathered round to watch (and photograph) the Mosos carrying out a scared ceremony in which they chanted incantations over the carcass and offered the tip of its heart to the gods. After this "picturesque" scene, it was back to work and within a week they had shot and strung up gorals of all sizes. Energized from the hunt, Roy wrote,

"There was a strange fascination about those mountains, and I thrilled with the thought that for twelve long months I was free to roam where I willed and explore their hidden mysteries." More pragmatically, he added later, "No dinner which I have ever eaten tasted like the one we had of goral steak that night and after a smoke I crawled into my sleeping bag, dead tired in body but with a happy heart."

Shortly thereafter, Roy developed a near-fatal infection in his hand. After weeks of devoted nursing by Yvette, he was back on his feet, but even then his "trigger finger" remained partially disabled. Heller and the Mosos continued to hunt during his illness, but the loss of Hotenfa's favorite dog during a particularly risky maneuver further delayed progress. The Andrews sympathized with Hotenfa's grief – the death of the dog was especially damaging to their own hunting prospects – and Roy wrote, "[Hotenfa] cried like a child and I am sure that he felt more real sorrow than he would have shown at the loss of his wife; for wives are much easier to get in China than good hunting dogs."

Once Roy had recovered, the band engaged another group of local hunters, this time Lolos, to supplement the ranks, and set off to collect specimens from the local serow population. The Lolos confounded their efforts. They were much feistier than the easygoing Mosos and seemed unimpressed by the museum team's flashy hunting kit. They also proved less willing to turn over animals they killed. Roy noted with much perplexity, "They preferred to hunt alone, although they recognized what an increased chance for game our high-power rifles gave them, and eventually left us while I was away on a short trip, even though we still owed them considerable money."

Abandoned by their Lolos and exhausted, the team threw in the towel at Snow Mountain, and began the multiple, complicated preparations to get the entire caravan to their next destination: the other side of the treacherous Yangtze River gorges. After tough trekking to the Yangtze, they found themselves in a situation akin to the famous riddle in which a farmer must ferry a wolf, a chicken and a bag of grain one-by-one across the river without any being eaten on the bank: getting their gear, mules and muleteers across the river without anything getting lost and stolen. The Andrews planned poorly, sending the team, the mules and most of the kit across first, saving the most valuable items to go across with them and Heller on the last ferry shipment. Much to their consternation, the ferry service closed just before they had a chance to cross, separating them from their muleteers and the bulk of their gear. All night was spent scowling across the gorge and conjecturing the damage their unsupervised staff had surely caused. All the worry was for naught, as their belongings were found safe and sound the next day.

Despite the difficulties it had caused them, they were impressed by the Yangtze Gorges, which they found even more stunning than the Grand Canyon. Roy enthusiastically noted: "If Yün-nan is ever made accessible by railroads this gorge should become a Mecca for tourists, for it is without doubt one of the most remarkable natural sights in the world."

Yvette found the natural beauty of their new Yangtze camp to be so breathtaking that she frantically rushed about snapping photos and recording film. Because of conditions on the trail, the film needed to be developed right away, and so, when not out with her camera, she spent her days holed up in her portable darkroom tent, a rubber cone suspended from a branch and sealed with stones. This was tedious and challenging work, especially given the lack of clean water, and holes in the "dark room" tent threatened the quality of the pictures. Roy marveled appreciatively:

"One who sits comfortably in a theatre or hall and sees moving-picture film which has been obtained in such remote parts of the world does not realize the difficulties in its preparation."

On the other hand, the hunting to be had at their new site was not as bountiful as they had hoped and they set off in search of new opportunities. The route traveled was along a well-beaten caravan path used by Tibetan tea traders, and the team was transfixed by these "picturesque, wild-looking natives". They wanted desperately to photograph the Tibetans they met on the road, but the Tibetans hated cameras and refused to pose. Bribes and pleading were ineffective, and the museum team eventually decided to resort to hunting tactics.

"What we could not get by bribery we tried to do by stealth and concealed ourselves behind bushes with the camera focused on a certain spot upon the road. The instant a Tibetan discovered it he would run like a frightened deer and in some mysterious way they seemed to have passed the word along that our camp was a spot to be avoided."

Although they managed to get a small amount of motion picture footage, their attempts to photo-document the Tibetans of Yunnan were largely unsuccessful.

After many more weeks of rambling around areas that bored them with lack of hunting opportunities, they stopped in Ta-li (Dali) before turning south. The hunting on this last stretch of northern Yunnan on their way back to Ta-li really perked up, and they spent several days joyously scrabbling across the stony hills chasing gorals. Roy was particularly elated by a hunt in which he very nearly skittered off the edge of a cliff, only to be saved in the nick of time by Hotenfa grabbing his sleeve. Roy went on to blast to smithereens the goral that had lured him into danger. The next day was Christmas Eve and, while the men were out hunting, Yvette gussied up the tent:

"[The tent] had been most wonderfully transformed. At the far end stood a Christmas tree, blazing with tiny candles and surrounded by masses of white cotton, through which shone red holly berries...Our Christmas dinner was a masterpiece. Four days previously I had shot a pair of mallard ducks and they formed the pièce de résistance. The dinner consisted of soup, ducks stuffed with chestnuts, currant jelly, baked squash, creamed carrots, chocolate cake, cheese and crackers, coffee and cigarettes."

After stuffing themselves, the team distributed gifts among their servants and then proceeded to round out the festivities by getting drunk on orange juice and bai jiu (Chinese rice liquor) cocktails.

Back in Ta-li, after the usual expat meet-and-greet, they overhauled their team and supplies, replacing most of their servants, including the unhappy "Woolworth Building". Once on the road again, they descended into the tropics, where they found a change in climate and also in the attitude of the locals, who were much warmer and more open. Wherever they went, they were welcomed by curious and gregarious crowds. At one village, the citizens lined the streets to greet the team:

"Just before camping the next day we passed through a large village where we were given a most flattering reception... The populace was out en masse to greet us and lined the streets three deep. It was a veritable triumphal entry and crowds of men and children followed us for half a mile outside the town, running beside our horses and staring with saucer-like eyes."

Pushing beyond populated areas and into the remote

rainforest, they found the wildlife of southern Yunnan to be as accommodating as the locals, and they set about trapping and shooting everything in sight. Roy straightforwardly laid out their plan of action in the region: "We forthwith decided to stay right where we were until this gold mine had been exhausted."

An excerpt from his journal describes an average day in camp:

"While I am away with the men [hunting], the lady of the camp works at her photography. I return in the late afternoon and after tea we wander through the woods together. It is the most delightful part of the day when the sun goes down and the shadows lengthen. We sit on a log in a small clearing where we can watch the upper branches of a splendid tree. It is the home of a great colony of red-bellied squirrels (Callosciurus erythraeus subsp.) and after a few moments of silence we see a flash of brown along a branch, my gun roars out, and there is a thud upon the ground...[Upon our return], the tents glow in the darkness like great yellow pumpkins. Ours is delightfully warmed by the charcoal brazier and, stretched comfortably on the beds, we write our daily records or read Dickens for half an hour."

Their idyllic life in the jungle carried on for several more weeks, but eventually, having collected hundreds of specimens, they had in fact "exhausted the gold mine", and so they decided to push further south. The forests became increasingly lush, which prompted Yvette to wonder "Could this really be China? Verily, it was a different China from that we had seen before! It might be Burma, India, Java, but never China!"

They stumbled upon civilization again at the trading post of Meng-ting and set up camp just below a monastery. Yvette was fascinated by the saffron-robed monks and occupied herself for several days trying to capture the "yellow flock of birds peering at us with bright round eyes" and "wrinkled bits of lemon peel".

Roy was decidedly less impressed: "They lead a lazy, worthless life, and from their sojourn in religious circles they learn only indolence and idleness."

At the weekly market however, the two were in agreement that the scene was stunning. The usually cynical Roy described the scene:

"[I was] in the midst of the most picturesque crowd of natives it has ever been my fortune to see. It was a group flashing with color, and every individual a study for an artist. There were blue-clad Chinese, Shans with tattooed legs, turbans of pink or white, and Burmans dressed in brilliant purple or green, Las, yellow-skinned Lisos, flat-faced Palaungs, Was, and Kachins in black and red strung about with beads or shells."

They spent market day frantically dashing around the town snapping photos and filming footage. No one at the market had ever seen either device before, but they showed little fear, and even became positively enthusiastic about allowing themselves to be captured on film after it was known that the Andrews paid cash for posed photographs.

After their Meng-ting market photo extravaganza, it was back into the jungle. Their guide at the newest camp was a tall, gangly and slow-moving Muslim Chinese man. Assuming him to be too sloth-like to be effective, they christened him "Dying Rabbit". Contrary to their expectations, he was not a dim-witted, slow-poke but a skilled hunter, who helped them to bring in quite a few jungle fowl (ancestor of the domestic barnyard chicken) and a steaming pile of fresh monkey skins. The monkeys they found particularly thrilling to hunt, with their near-human intelligence and mannerisms. Roy describes one hunt in particular:

"[The monkey's voice] vibrated an instant, filling all the forest with its richness, and slowly died away. Again and again it floated over the tree-tops and we listened strangely moved, for it was like the music of an exquisite contralto voice…I fired a charge of B.B.'s at the lowest branch [and got one]."

After they had blasted a satisfactory number of monkeys from the trees, they bade farewell to "Dying Rabbit" and, on his advice, headed for a village called Ma-li-ling. What should have been a morning's trip dragged on for over a day when their native guide got hopelessly lost. Having strayed far from their intended path, the Andrews became paranoid that they had crossed illegally into Burma. These fears were realized several hours later, when their guide took them traipsing through several tell-tale fields of poppies. (Growing poppies was illegal in China by the time, as the authorities tried to curb the nation's opium addiction, but it was still common practice in Burma.)

Crossing into Burma was highly problematic, because they had no permits for hunting in the country and, more importantly, because it was during World War I and Burma was British territory. It was dangerous to enter illegally with such a large armed party. Aware of this, the mule drivers attempted to extort money from the Andrews in exchange for their discretion and aid in getting them back into China quietly and safely. An outraged Roy rejected their demands and reacted with swift violence: "Taking his Mannlicher rifle, Roy called the mafus [mule drivers] together and told them that if any man touched a load he would begin to shoot the mules and that if they made the slightest resistance the gun would be turned on them."

Keeping the mule drivers under armed guard, the Andrews and Heller decided that – in order to spite the mule drivers and avoid them seeking revenge – they would turn themselves in at the nearest military installment and leave their fate in the hands of the Burmese authorities.

At the military base, rather than being punished, the Andrews and Heller were welcomed with open arms by a homesick British officer named Captain Clive.

"[Clive] was as clean-shaved and well-groomed as though he had been expecting us for days and the tiffin to which we sat down was as dainty and well served as it could have been in the midst of civilization."

Besides pampering them with delights from "back home", Clive also gave them fresh news of the war, and they learned that, since they had entered the jungle, the United States had broken diplomatic ties with Germany. Although technically prisoners of war, the team enjoyed a luxurious period of rest and relaxation in Clive's Burmese villa while awaiting clearance to proceed from the authorities in Rangoon. The ingenious but slow heliograph communication system used ("With mirrors during the day and lanterns at night messages were flashed from one mountain top to another and, under favourable conditions, reached Lashio in seven or eight hours") delayed the process, and it was over a week before they were "freed". Yvette said upon their release, "If we are ever again made 'prisoners of war' we hope our captor will be as delightful a gentleman as Captain Clive."

After their release, the team headed straight back into China, rolling up their sleeves almost immediately after crossing the border and spending several days hunting peacocks on the shores of the Salween River. The peacocks were wily birds, and the team left the area with the corpses of only one shriveled old female and a few babies.

Their poor luck continued and they faced many trials over the following weeks. First, they found themselves on a plain that was "as uninteresting to the zoölogist as it could possibly be." Next, Roy caught malaria and was out of commission for several days. Then the mail was delayed. They scowled their way through the town where their mail should have been, grumpily setting up yet another jungle camp – which was promptly flooded. Eventually they found a hunting ground loaded with plump monkeys and went on a shooting rampage. Roy again narrowly cheated death, this time by surviving a fall down a sheer cliff face and catching his rifle strap on a twig. (He had been trying to single-handedly haul a large monkey corpse to camp.)

Deciding not to push their luck, the team skinned the monkeys and began to prepare to leave China for good, heading directly for Teng-Yueh, a border crossing with India. After arriving, they spent many days traipsing between tea parties and tennis engagements with the expats. They even played golf on a course that had been rather distastefully set up in a Chinese cemetery. However, it was not all fun and games, as, while there, they learned that the United States had joined the war. As a result, they needed to reevaluate the logistics of their trip home. Roy and Yvette also purchased two bear cubs in Teng-Yueh, intending to keep them as pets, and needed to make the corresponding travel arrangements. (One of the bears didn't survive the trip, but the other made it back to the States and lived with the Andrews' in New York for several years before being donated to the National Zoo in Washington, DC.)

With most of their onward arrangements settled, the team decided to go for one last big game hunt before heading home. One of their hosts in Teng-Yueh was a skilled marksman, who led them to fertile hunting grounds. While the game population was large, the steep rocky terrain made things challenging. Roy and Heller discovered that it was possible to use their long range rifles to easily pick off the animals from the other side of the canyon, and quickly bagged dozens. Roy conceded that this was "unsportsmanlike" but argued that, as it was being done in the name of "Science" it could be allowed. Nonetheless, he and Heller returned to the canyons to hunt like "gentlemen". Roy struggled in spotting game among the boulders, but his local guides could pick them out easily. Not one to allow the "natives" to one-up him, he reasoned the situation thus:

"Their eyes had never been dimmed by study and I suppose were as keen as those of primitive man who possibly hunted gorals or their relatives thousands of years ago over these same hills."

In a fittingly dramatic finale to this last hunt, Roy blasted a massive serow off a cliff and into a river. In order to recover the dead animal, he needed to swim across whitewater rapids and scale a steep cliff. After drafting in a reluctant Chinese woodcutter to assist, the two stripped down and swam the river, eventually getting the animal back up the cliff. However, the porter with their clothing had vanished, and Roy and the hunter had to hike back to camp "with only the proverbial smile and minus even the necktie." Roy was mortified, reporting that at one point "a Chinese woman suddenly appeared over a little hill. I dived into the tall ferns beside the road, burrowing like a rabbit."

After the final hunt (and after Roy was reunited with his clothes), it was time for the expedition to pack their bags. This was no small task. They had collected, among other things, the remains of over 2,100 mammals and 800 birds, as well as 500 photographic plates and 10,000 feet of film. The packing procedures were of utmost urgency, because the animal specimens needed to be dried and placed in airtight containers before the summer rains set in, which was accomplished with little time to spare. Equipped with their final set of porters, they turned towards Burma and India, and immediately noticed a marked improvement:

"What a difference between the country we were leaving and the one we were about to enter! It is the "deadly parallel" of the old East and the new West. On the one side is China with her flooded roads and bridges of rotting timber, the outward and visible signs of a nation still living in the Middle Ages, fighting progress, shackled by the iron doctrines of Confucius to the long dead past. Across the river is English Burma, with eyes turned forward, ever watchful of the welfare of her people, her iron bridges and macadam roads representing the very essence of modern thought and progress."

Nonetheless, the entire team – including the ever-macho Roy – shed tears at this departure, and when they entered the British colonial city of Bhamo, they felt "strange and shy" being back in "proper civilization". Despite their praise for the British colony's modernity, it seems their travel difficulties began anew once they left China, spending the next several months zigzagging across India in order to reach a port from which they could return to New York. It was decided that traveling via the Atlantic would be impossible, and so they headed back to Hong Kong (via Singapore), and then Japan, San Francisco and finally New York, where the specimens were unloaded at the museum and the journey finished.

With America now at war, their homecoming was much more restrained than their raucous departure had been. For a man who seemed to find Chinese civilization utterly distressing and disgusting, and a nightmare for travelers, Roy concluded the tale of their journeys on a surprisingly reflective and sentimental note:

"The story of our travels is at an end. Once more we are indefinable units in a vast work-a-day world, bound by the iron chains of convention to the customs of civilized men and things. The glorious days in our beloved East are gone, and yet, to us, the Orient seems not far away, for the miles of land and water can be traversed in a thought. Again we stand before our tent with the fragrant breath of the pines about us, watching the glistening peaks of the Snow Mountain turn purple and gold in the setting sun; again, we feel the mystic spell of the jungle, or hear the low, sweet tones of a gibbon's call. We have only to shut our eyes to bring back a picture of the bleak barriers of the Forbidden Land or the sunlit streets of a Burma village. Thank God, we saw it all together and such blessed memories can never die."

www.ingramcontent.com/pod-product-compliance
Lightning Source LLC
Chambersburg PA
CBHW011237120626
46549CB00009B/3298